How to Believe in God

CLARK STRAND

HOW TO BELIEVE IN GOD

WHETHER YOU BELIEVE IN RELIGION OR NOT

DOUBLEDAY

New York London Toronto Sydney Auckland

DD

DOUBLEDAY

Published in the United States by Doubleday, an imprint of The
Doubleday Publishing Group, a division of Random House, Inc.,
New York.
www.doubleday.com

DOUBLEDAY is a registered trademark and the DD colophon is a
trademark of Random House, Inc.

LIBRARY OF CONGRESS CATALOGING-IN-PUBLICATION DATA
Strand, Clark, 1957–
   How to believe in God (whether you believe in religion or not) /
by Clark Strand. — 1st ed.
        p. cm.
1. Bible—Criticism, interpretation, etc. 2. Apologetics.
3. Christianity and other religions—Buddhism. 4. Buddhism—
Relations—Christianity. I. Title.
   BS511.3.S78 2008
   220.6—dc 22

                          2008006645

ISBN 978-0-7679-2069-8

PRINTED IN THE UNITED STATES OF AMERICA

10 9 8 7 6 5 4 3 2 1

FIRST EDITION

For my father, Allan E. Strand Jr.,

who gave me the Bible.

And for my mother, Anne W. Strand,

who taught me to seek God.

God builds his temple in the heart

on the ruins of churches and religions.

—RALPH WALDO EMERSON

Contents

Acknowledgments

How to Believe in God (Whether You Believe in Religion or Not) was an extremely difficult book to write, and I doubted for many years that I would ever be able to finish it. That I was able, and that you are now holding it in your hands, says much about my friends and family.

First among those who are responsible for the book's creation and conception are the members of our Woodstock Bible Study Group, who have met every Thursday night for the past eight years to read the Bible for its questions, and not just its answers—a process that has required of them not only great faith and great doubt, but also great endurance. For spiritual friendship, inspiration, and encouragement of every kind, I am indebted to them all, but especially to James Lignori, whose commitment, both to the group and to the book it ultimately produced, was simply absolute; and to Priscilla Lignori, who documented our meetings with painstaking care, raising questions that in many cases had only been hinted at during the meetings themselves and taking them even further. It is no exaggeration to say that because of her our meetings never really ended, but ran together week after week as a continuously unfolding conversation between spiritual friends. I am blessed to have such partners for the years of work ahead.

To the list of those who have contributed the most to our group in recent years, and therefore to the book, I would add Davida Libman, whose inspired yearlong reading of the book of Job changed the way I think about the rest of the Bible; Jim and Carla Potter, who infused our meetings with unexpected cultural riches and brought with them a lifetime of insight gained as psychotherapists at precisely the moment it was needed; Denise Ranaghan, who insisted that our discussions serve the needs of each member and helped us to realize with even greater clarity that, going forward, religion must be made to serve life, not vice versa; and Susan Manuso, who stretched the thread of our Woodstock conversations as far as California without ever letting it go. I cannot believe that I deserve such friends, but I accept them with gratitude.

The following group members each made profound contributions over the years as well; the book is theirs as much as mine: Stephanie Barnes, Dimitri Hernandez, Linda Mandano, Barbara Sarah, Marty LaForse, Sarah Berk, Larry Berk, Reverend Philip Washburn, Nancy Washburn, Frank Jude, Bruce Jackson, Duff Allen, Julia Indichova, Angela Stockwell, Julie Stebbens, Corinne Mol, Joanne Rowley, Art Sherman, Gioia Timpanelli, and Laurie Ylvisaker. In addition, the first version of *How to Believe in God* was written to be read aloud at the weekly meeting of the Koans of the Bible Study Group in St. Paul, Minnesota, where I traveled to teach for some years at the invitation of my friends Natalie Goldberg and Dosho Mike Port of the Clouds in Water Zen Center. Particular thanks are owed to Bob Keim and Sheila Moriarity for their continuing support and sponsorship of that group.

Finally, three other members of our Woodstock group warrant special mention. David Tapper is a source of continual inspiration and a treasured family friend. At age eighty, he is the most relentless yet open-minded spiritual explorer I have ever known. It was Dave who suggested I start these groups in the first place, and Dave who first conceived of the title of this book. Likewise, Andrea Barrist Stern has been a mainstay and "Great Mother," both to the group and to our family, for nearly a decade. Our gratitude to her knows no bounds. Finally, many of the spiritual lessons I discovered in writing *How to Believe in God* came by way of Robert Esformes, whose knowledge of Jewish mysticism is encyclopedic. Without these three, our lives would be infinitely poorer.

Beyond our weekly group, there were countless individuals—monks, nuns, priests, and ordinary believers—who shared their most treasured spiritual teachings with me, knowing all the while that I was not likely to use them in a way that was consistent with the norms of their traditions. Despite their desires to convert me in the beginning, in the end I believe they contributed out of pure generosity of heart. How else can I explain why, on a hot summer day, a group of Hasidic rabbis spent the entire afternoon cheerfully explaining their method of solitary prayer to a non-Jewish visitor who stumbled into their shul wearing shorts, sandals, sunglasses, and a Hawaiian shirt? Or why a woman from the Jehovah's Witnesses would come to my house once a week for three months straight to teach me how the Witnesses read the Bible? Or, for that matter, why an Afghan refugee who confessed to me that he was too nervous in post-9/11 Manhattan to discuss his faith with anyone nevertheless taught me to use the *tesbih* beads of his tradition to call on Allah's name? It must have been clear to everyone that I had no intention of becoming a Muslim, a Jehovah's Witness, an Orthodox Christian, or a Hasidic Jew. My only regret in my relationships with these individuals is that some of them—in particular, the Christian bookstore owner in Kingston, New York, to whom I am more indebted than anyone else—still worry over the state of my soul. In such cases, I can answer only that the profound gratitude I feel toward each of them warrants its own kind of protection in the eyes of God.

There are others I am able to thank openly, though some have since passed on. These are Lex Hixon, Father Basil Pennington, Sister Benedicta of the Convent of St. Helena, Dovid Krafchow, Rabbi Jonathan Kligler, Hoshin and Josephine Seki, Taitetsu and Alice Unno, Reverend T. K. Nakagaki, Masao Yokota, Bill Aiken, Ethan Gelbaum, Chance O'Connor, Jack Slockbower, and Andrew Gebert. Special thanks are due to Father Tom Miller of the Cathedral of St. John the Divine, who served as my spiritual adviser for a number of years, and to my close friend and the godfather of my children, Thanissaro Bhikkhu, Abbot of Metta Forest Monastery, with whom I have shared every other thought that passed through my head for years now. He is not to be blamed for any of them, but with the exception of my wife, Perdita, in most cases he was the first to hear them. Additionally, Daisaku Ikeda, President of Soka Gakkai International, has been a great inspiration to me. The opportunities for study and travel afforded by my friendship with the Soka Gakkai have given me the chance to watch a global religion in the process of being born, for which I am deeply grateful. Finally, though thanks alone are small compensation for the pains he took with me over the fourteen years of our association, I must express my deepest appreciation to Eido Tai Shimano Roshi, Abbot of Dai Bosatsu Zendo. Though it seems strange to offer a book on the Bible as evidence that his Zen teachings were not in vain, more than anything else I have written, *How to Believe in God* is a testament to those teachings, and the debt I owe him is visible, to me at least, on every page.

A woman I often shared a café table with over the past decade once remarked that I always seemed to be reading some little book on prayer. "Is it the same book," she asked me one day, "or a different one each time?"

"The same book," I replied, "only written by different authors."

The "little books" I consulted in writing *How to Believe in God* are far too numerous to name. Some I returned to so often, however, that the debt I owe them simply must be acknowledged. Among these were Shinran's *Tannisho*, translated by Taitetsu Unno; *Plain Words on the Pure Land Way*, translated by Dennis Hirota; *Thus Have I Heard* and *The Evil Person*, both by Shuichi Maida, translated by Nobuo Haneda; *The Great Natural Way*, by the Venerable Hozen Seki; and *Buddha of Infinite Light: The Teachings of Shin Buddhism*, by D. T. Suzuki. Each of these is a masterpiece of Buddhist thought and, though all but the last can be difficult to come by, they are well worth the effort required to track them down. In addition, I read constantly from Burton Watson's translation of *The Lotus Sutra* and from both volumes of *The Writings of Nichiren Daishonin*, the collected letters of the thirteenth-century Japanese saint who, probably alone in all of Buddhism, deserves the biblical title "prophet."

Apart from these, I would add one small but extraordinary text from the Jewish tradition: Rebbe Nachman's *Outpouring of the Soul*, translated by the late Rabbi Aryeh Kaplan and published by the Breslov Research Institute. I am also particularly indebted to Ibn Al-'Arabi's *101 Diamonds from the Oral Tradition of the Glorious Messenger Muhammad*, translated and interpreted by Lex Hixon and Fariha Al-Jerrahi, and to *The Gospel of Sri Ramakrishna*, the abridged version of which was like carrying a miracle around in my coat pocket.

The Catholic and Orthodox Christian texts I consulted ran to the hundreds. The most important of these, however, were *Some Minor Works of Richard Rolle*, sadly now almost impossible to come by; *Revelations of Divine Love*, by Julian of Norwich; E. Kadloubovsky and G. E. H. Palmer's one-volume work *Writings from the Philokalia on Prayer of the Heart*; and Father Lev Gillet's gemlike devotional classic *On the Invocation of the Name of Jesus*.

My readings in contemporary Protestantism were too varied and too numerous and occurred over too long a period of time for me to remember them all now, and included a great many tracts, pamphlets, and individual sermons I have long since lost track of. Where, for instance, did I first hear Abraham described as "a ball in a groove" when he leads the boy Isaac up Mount Moriah? Sadly, I can no longer remember. But I would be remiss if I did not acknowledge my debt to the many traditional resources for Bible study in that tradition, and especially to the publishers of the *Thompson Chain-Reference Study Bible*, which still stands as a monument to American biblical literacy, even in this age of Google, Wikipedia, and BibleGateway.com. That book was always my first and final resource in writing *How to Believe in God.*

Last of all, I wish to thank those who "made the book happen." For financial assistance at various times during the years it took to complete: my grandmother, Lois Walker; my brother, Allan Strand, and his wife, Maureen; my parents, Anne and Allan Strand; my natural father, Bob Weigel, and his wife, Connie; Andrea Barrist Stern; James and Priscilla Lignori; and Jim and Carla Potter. Likewise, apart from members of our study group, most of whom read the book as I wrote it (including James and Priscilla, Jim and Carla, Phil Washburn, Gioia Timpanelli, Robert Esformes, David Tapper, Andrea Barrist Stern, Stephanie Barnes, and Susan Manuso), the following friends and family members reviewed it in its final manuscript form and offered valuable advice: Susan Rudnick, Beckie Kravetz, Alan Weisman, Bar Scott, Michele Slung, Anne Fagan, Mark Finn, Matthew Finn, Tom Lund, Tom Miller, Linda Dickey, Bruce and Diana Cobbold, and Beth Lipton. Linda Dickey, in particular, has offered friendship, feedback, and more than a few pep talks over the years when I needed them most. And Tom Lund must be acknowledged as my "silent partner" in the final phase of the writing. That I was able to complete the book at all is largely due to his support and loving advice. Heartfelt appreciation is also due to my northern family: to my beloved brother-in-law, Mark Finn; his wife, Michal; and my nephews Adam and Daniel, with whom I have shared so much good food, good wine, and good talk over the years. I don't know where I'd be without their constant love and support. Finally, for friendship, laughter, and the encouragement to go on: Sparrow and Ellen Carter, Liz and Vinnie Martucci, Tom and Debbie Carpenter, Mark and Nancy Lerner, Pia and James Lasdun, Jim Hoffman, Kathy Nolan, and Mark Rogisin—to which list I must also add Jeff Cuiule, Audrey Cusson, and Shana Cutler of Mirabai Books for their continued friendship and (along with the Woodstock Dutch Reformed Church) for providing space for our weekly meetings. Likewise, special thanks to Barry Samuels and Ellen Shapiro of the Golden Notebook: independent booksellers enlighten the hearts and nourish the souls of small progressive communities; may they endure forever.

My agent Geri Thoma championed this project from the beginning, showing remarkable patience and resilience as it passed through various incarnations with different editors and publishers. Amy Hertz of Riverhead first saw the potential for *How to Believe in God* and trusted me enough as a writer to allow vast swaths of time to get it done. Andrew Corbin of Doubleday Religion shepherded the book through the editorial process; Greg Mollica went well beyond the call of duty in getting the cover just right; and Trace Murphy, John Burke, Darya Porat, and Rosalie Wieder kept four or five balls in the air simultaneously and never dropped one. In the end, Gary Jensen arrived on the scene as the book's final editor, inheriting the responsibility for figuring out how best to share it with the world, a task he took up with an enthusiasm that, probably because he is a religious author himself, reflected a feel for the book that would have been worthy of its acquiring editor. In all, I feel quite blessed.

Those, then, are the people I can thank, and in doing so can in some small measure repay for their kindness in helping *How to Believe in God* become a reality. But there are three others for whom thanks alone can hardly be sufficient.

I cannot possibly express the debt I owe to my wife, soul mate, and fellow author, Perdita Finn. *How to Believe in God (Whether You Believe in Religion or Not)* was a journey we made together. The thoughts, the insights, and whatever poetry are contained herein are the relic of an ongoing conversation—about life, love, the Bible, and everything in between—held over coffee, over breakfast, across the table where we write together each and every day, while driving to swim meets with our children, or whispered to each other in the dead of night with no one to hear but God. That conversation is the inspiration and the joy of my life, and though I make no special claims for reincarnation in this book, it seems inconceivable that it began only when we first met over coffee at the Hungarian Pastry Shop in Manhattan all those years ago. Even in those first moments, it felt like the time before we knew each other was simply another pause, after which one says, "You know, I've been thinking . . ."

To my extraordinary children, Sophie Strand and Jonah Strand, who arrived in the middle of that conversation and therefore cannot remember a time when their mother and I were *not* working on *How to Believe in God*, I owe a debt of gratitude I can never repay. They were my inspiration from the start. This book belongs to them and to their children in a way that it will never belong to me. Their lives are already a testament to its message of universal salvation, which they accept as a matter of course, as if it were a point too obvious to argue. The future rests with them.

A Buddhist

Returns to the Bible

Tell me about the God you don't believe in. Is it the God who separates the saved from the damned, reserving bliss for the blessed, and brimstone for the nonbeliever? Or perhaps the narrow-minded God who resists new ways of thinking, the God who will brook no question and no discourse, the one who prefers the world the way it was before feminism or civil rights, before the discovery of evolution and quantum physics or the creation and collapse of stars? Is it the God who sponsors crusades, jihads, and pogroms? Or maybe the one who tells a twenty-four-year-old man with a wife and three children to blow himself up in a crowded public square?

The list could go on and on. There's the God who created the world in six days. And then there's the one who puts a beautiful fruit tree within reach of his children, forbids them on pain of death to eat from it, then promptly disappears to some other part of the garden, keeping an eye peeled behind the bushes to see what they will do. There's the one with a rule for everything from menstruation to shellfish, who strikes people dead when they cross him. And then there's the one who kills Egyptian babies in order to save Jewish ones, then sends his only son to save all of mankind (so long as they are willing to become Christian). The Bible itself is filled with Gods we don't believe in. Or with ones who *shouldn't* be believed in.

Where did these Gods come from, and what are we to do with them now that they are here? Is there any way to reform or reeducate them? Is there any way to get through to them with the message that the world is bigger and more inclusive now than in the days of desert and tribe? And if not—if, as many modern atheists claim, the world is better off without them—what, if anything, is there to replace them with? Are we destined to live with "a God-shaped hole" at the center of our being? However many problems these troubled Gods created, those societies who succeeded in ousting them have hardly fared better. The loss of God in modern society has made totalitarianism in all its many forms, from communist to corporate, a virtual inevitability of modern life. True, the old God might have been a problem, but nonbelief doesn't seem to be an option. "We are born believing," wrote Ralph Waldo Emerson. "A man bears beliefs as a tree bears apples." In the absence of God, human beings will always find *something* to believe in: science, progress, money, or just the ever-increasing power of the self.

So where does that leave us now?

Oddly enough, right where we started—with the God of the Bible, as mysterious and difficult to account for as he is.

During the years I was working on this book, any number of people had occasion to ask me: Why the Bible? Why go back through all those plagues and rules? Why endure all the bloodletting and barbarism of an earlier, more primitive era—an era when people thought demons caused diseases, women were unclean during their periods, and homosexuality was an abomination before God? Why not start over with a fresh slate and write about a God who *is* worth believing in? But the answer to those questions, while surprising, was also very simple: because going back into the Bible is the same as going back into ourselves.

For most Westerners, God *lives* in the Bible. For better or worse, we can't change our idea of God without changing our ideas about the Bible first. And this is true for everyone in our society, whether they were raised in a religiously observant household or not. The Bible is the spiritual matrix of Western culture, the point of origin for all of our deepest beliefs and hopes and fears. It is the source of many of our laws and customs, not to mention many of our everyday expressions and the mind-set that comes along with them. It is the origin even of our ideas of time, from the seven days of the week to the "beginning" and the "end" of the world. You may not read it, or even know what it says, and still the Bible is inside of you. It's in the air we breathe, and it's in the culture at large. And therefore the idea of God is in us, too. There is no escaping it.

That was what I discovered in the end, and the reason I came back to the Bible in the effort to find a God I could believe in. And when I found that God, I discovered he'd been there all along. Granted, I had to learn to read the Bible in a completely different way than it is read by most religious people. But that was the journey I had to take. I tried any number of other routes along the way, most of them an effort to circumvent the Bible altogether, and some of them going in the opposite direction.

In the years following 1990, when I stopped being a Buddhist monk, I devoted myself to literally dozens of different spiritual disciplines, from Jewish meditation to the Muslim practice of calling on the ninety-nine names of God. At one time or another, I taught *A Course in Miracles*; practiced the Catholic rosary with all its various prayers and mysteries;

combined the ancient words of the Jesus prayer with my breathing, then my heartbeat; said the *nembutsu* (the name of Amida Buddha) as many as thirty thousand times a day until, as with the Jesus prayer, eventually it came to say itself. I rose from sleep to do *hitbodedut*, the Hasidic practice of free-form meditation performed out of doors in the middle of the night by speaking aloud to God. I recited the Psalms, the Qur'an, and the Lotus Sutra, and memorized portions of each so that I could say them anywhere, at any time.

And that's just the beginning.

An exhaustive list would go on for several pages, including various other forms of prayer, meditation, visualization, and the like. The only feature of the spiritual life I was never able to become very disciplined about was going to church, although I tried for many years. Since earliest childhood, despite the fact that I was raised in a religious southern household (or maybe because of it), I have never liked hymns.

As a child I remember experiencing church as a mildly oppressive affair involving long periods of forced stillness, punctuated by flashes of something meaningful that were, however, extremely hard to get a good glimpse at. My relationship to God, by comparison, was a clean, true line. I believed in him and prayed each night without being prompted.

Now I lay me down to sleep.
I pray the Lord my soul to keep.
If I should die before I wake
I pray the Lord my soul to take.

I can't remember whether I identified "Lord" with Jesus or with God—I don't recall distinguishing much between them. Whoever the Lord was, he watched over your soul while you slept and was capable of keeping track of it even if you died. This thought deeply impressed me as a child.

My grandfather had passed away when my mother was thirteen, six years before I was born, and although I had never known him, it was one of those cases where a person is more present for his absence. His premature death from heart disease loomed over my childhood like those early winter dusks that came on so suddenly they barely left time to get back home before dark. And so it was this aspect of the prayer that impressed me most—that beyond the edges of waking consciousness, beyond the frame, as it were, of life itself, there was someone or something there. Naturally, I didn't think of it in those terms exactly, but that is what I felt.

It is important to understand up front that, when it comes to belief in God, no one develops much beyond the age of three or four years old. Our spiritual beliefs may evolve, becoming more complex or sophisticated, but that most basic, most singular belief—in an eternal reality beyond the reaches of the self—does not develop. It's a simple mechanism, like a life jacket or a ladder. The effort to develop or systematize it nearly always has the effect of obscuring it in the end. That is why Jesus advised his disciples to become like little children if they would enter the kingdom of God, and the reason why the Japanese Buddhist saint Honen once said, "The moment a scholar is born, he forgets the Buddha's name." I don't believe for a moment that Honen was talking only about those who study religion in an academic or theological setting. He was referring to the basic human tendency to forget what is most simple and true.

We all do this, myself included. I don't remember exactly where along the way I lost my simplicity. It isn't something we part with willingly, knowing what we do. What I do remember is sitting in Sunday school one morning as a teenager and asking the teachers, an insurance salesman and his wife, where specifically in the Bible it said that America was right to go to war with Vietnam, or that blacks should never marry whites. They thought I was just out to make trouble, and perhaps I was, but once I started asking such questions, it was impossible to stop. A few

Sundays later my father, who had always insisted that I attend church with the family, told me he thought I had reached the age where I could decide for myself whether or not to go. Besides which, he knew I hated the hymns.

By the time I entered college, there was nothing left of the faith I'd grown up with. I realize now how easy it is to confuse church with God. Most of us grow up believing that religion and God are essentially the same (or ought to be), when in fact, they may have nothing to do with each other. In retrospect, I'm not sure I ever really lost my belief in God. It was religion I no longer believed in. And I thought that also meant I couldn't believe in God.

Religion took a hard fall. In college I read about the Crusades, the Spanish Inquisition, and countless Christian pogroms against the Jews. I discovered that popes had lied and sanctioned murder, that Martin Luther was an anti-Semite, and that the strongest opponents of the civil rights movement had been the God-fearing men and women I'd brushed knees with in church from the moment I first sat in a pew. I read books about the Bible and discovered that it hadn't been written by God or Moses or the direct disciples of Jesus. It was a book like any other, for which there was ultimately no more moral authority than there was for Edith Hamilton's *Mythology* or the fairy tales of the Brothers Grimm— or so I thought at the time.

So great was my disenchantment with religion, in fact, that about a year later, when the experience of belief finally came, I didn't recognize it for what it was. My glimpse at the eternal lasted only for a fraction of a second, but its effects were with me for weeks thereafter as a deeply settled feeling, a trust that all was well and always had been, that in all the universe there was not one cause for worry or alarm.

Because I had rejected Christianity, it never occurred to me to identify that experience with God. Like many other people who grew up during the sixties and seventies, I had read books on Eastern philosophy and religion. And so it was to Buddhism I turned for an explanation of what had happened, and it was there, driven by the relentless energy of conversion, that my adult religious education began.

I say *religious* education, not spiritual, because from the very beginning my experience of Buddhism was characterized by a phenomenon I call *half-belief,* and half-belief has everything to do with religion and nothing to do with Buddha or with God.

Half-believers aspire to believe in God or Buddha, Allah or Avalokiteshvara, and take on the *guise* of belief (with its attendant attitudes, behaviors, and other norms), but in truth they still feel unsettled in their hearts, which is no doubt why they are often so intent on turning up the volume on religion, bringing it to the forefront of their political and social life. Half-believers seek some confirmation in the external world to complete an internal process that remains half finished within them, and among other things that usually means denying the truth or efficacy of other religious paths.

Not long after I became a Buddhist my family took a trip to Philadelphia, where, before he met my mother, my father had enrolled at West-minister Theological Seminary. Although it wasn't clear to me at the time, I think my father, having recognized the stirrings of spiritual awareness in my life, wanted to share something of his own experience as a young seminarian. Although he ultimately hadn't become a minister, he nevertheless thought of those years as having determined the future direction of his life.

Of course, I wouldn't hear any of it—I was a half-believer from the start. My Buddhism relied on the certainty that God did not exist, and therefore that anything associated with him, including my father's religious experiences as a young man, was at best a quaint fiction, at worst a willful self-deception. It is hard to believe now that I could have been so callous, but at the time I was convinced that Buddhism alone held the answer, and therefore that Christianity did not.

I began meditating several hours a day, wore *mala* beads, and threw out my mattress and box springs, replacing them with a futon on the floor. Eventually I left my first marriage, gave away all my money, and moved into a Zen monastery with only the clothes on my back and what possessions could fit in an army duffel bag. Still it wasn't enough. Half-belief never is. And so finally I became a monk. And when *that* didn't work, I took over a large temple in Manhattan and began to teach Zen to others. At that point, there was nowhere left to go. My thirty-third year found me dressed in a black robe with a shaved head, on the verge of becoming a Zen master in my own right—all this without the most basic requirement for any religious life.

It was the lie of it all that got to me in the end—the gradual but inevitable realization that, whatever my teacher and fellow Buddhists might be telling me about my level of attainment, Zen had been little more than an elaborate game of spiritual dress-up. I was no different than I had been before. The countless hours of meditation had made me a little less anxious, a bit more connected to the here and now. And, of course, I'd mastered a great deal of religious ritual and terminology. But it hadn't given me back the peace of mind I had briefly experienced at nineteen. Some years later, remarried and with two children, I had a dramatic demonstration of this fact on board a flight out of Memphis, Tennessee.

Not long after takeoff an electrical fire in the cockpit caused smoke to enter the cabin, after which the plane immediately went into a dive. We later learned that the pilot had followed an emergency directive to get the plane back on the ground as quickly as possible, but at the time everyone, including all the flight attendants, clearly believed we would die.

Had I still been single at the time, and still a monk, a Buddhist prayer might have risen to my lips at that moment. But when my four-year-old daughter reached her hand across the aisle to hold mine, and said, "Daddy, are we going to die?" it was the name of Jesus I called in my heart. It was like one of those dreams where you suddenly discover a room in your house you never knew was there. I was granted a brief glimpse into the room of the heart and found that it was just as I had always secretly feared: I wasn't a Buddhist after all. But then, Jesus notwithstanding, I wasn't exactly a Christian either, and hadn't been for a long, long time.

That was the beginning of a ten-year period in my life during which I searched the religious traditions of the world for something to believe in again. Before that plane ride out of Memphis, I had always considered myself a Zen Buddhist. Afterward, I didn't know what I was anymore. I'd gone too far into Buddhism to come back to the Christianity I'd grown up with, far enough to know that the claims of any religion to hold the exclusive patent on God were not only false but, indeed, represented the very worst impulse religion had to offer. To put it plainly, my spiritual life had come unmoored.

Although my experience aboard that plane was perhaps unique, the reality it laid bare is all too common. That same feeling of spiritual dislocation characterizes the experience of many people in the current age. At the turn of the twenty-first century, it is more difficult to believe in God than ever before. No longer is there one book (the Bible), no longer one theology, one local priest or rabbi. No longer is there one prevailing religious worldview. We live in a world on the brink of a great transition, and that transition, more than anything, concerns our idea of God.

The problem of God for people living in a postmodern age is no longer merely the problem of scientific and historical inquiry, as it was during the nineteenth and twentieth centuries; it is the problem of multiculturalism—the inevitable clash of ideologies that has accompanied jet travel, the Internet, political inclusivism, and the global economy. But those ideologies clash only so long as they refuse to be informed by one another. For a tribal God—a God kept tightly sealed inside the box of a culturally constructed ideology—is, as the Bible itself often shows us, a violent, warlike God.

Some years ago, in the midst of my ongoing effort to find a God I *could* believe in, I discovered the teachings of Pure Land Buddhism, and in those teachings I at last found the spiritual key that unlocked the treasure chest of the Bible. The Pure Land tradition spoke of two powerful forces at work in human life. But those forces weren't good and evil, as I'd always been taught. Good and evil were real enough, according to Pure Land Buddhism, but they weren't the root problem of human life. There was a more primal choice that always came into play before them. The Pure Land masters taught that it was Self Power and Other Power that warred for our souls.

As a way of understanding Self Power and Other Power, we can think of the difference between falling forward and falling back. If we fall forward, we can always catch ourselves simply by putting one foot forward. In fact, that is exactly what we do in walking. We fall forward and catch ourselves—over and over again. From earliest memory, that is how we have accomplished most things in life, walking here or there under our own steam, doing whatever it is we do. This is Self Power—getting where we need to go in life by our own wits, living by our resources alone—and as modern human beings we have extended its range to a degree unimaginable to even the most forward-thinking people of previous centuries. We can control everything from the global climate (albeit unintentionally) to the beating of our own hearts.

But what about falling back? When we fall backward it is impossible to catch ourselves, no matter how scientifically or technologically advanced we become, no matter how far we extend the range of those things we can manipulate. To fall back we must have the sense that there is someone there to catch us, some Other Power to save us when we cannot save ourselves; otherwise, we will never do it. We will never trust completely in life itself, never experience true freedom, never let ourselves go.

This would be no problem if it weren't for the fact that we all fall anyway in the end. Even if our lives go well and we somehow manage to negotiate life's more commonplace heartaches and disasters, eventually we will reach the place where we can go no further. Advanced as we may be compared with people who lived at the time of Jesus or Buddha, we still live in denial of this simplest of all existential facts: we will die. Eventually all that we love, and all that we hold to by way of belief or conviction, will simply pass away. And the self we have constructed and maintained and believed in more than anything, making it the center of our reality as thinking beings, will dissolve as quickly as a waking dream. I am reminded of a verse from the Psalms that reads: "His breath goeth forth, he returneth to his earth; in that very day his thoughts perish" (Psalm 146:4).*

As long as we are convinced that we can save ourselves, we will use every means at our disposal to do so—even spiritual means. We will attempt to do good deeds and avoid evil ones, not for their own sake, or out of love for God, but as part of a calculated bargain, and this, finally, is the essence of half-belief. Were it a matter of those who believed and those who did not, there would be no problem, but half-belief—which carries the liabilities of both and the benefits of neither—is the most dangerous form of religious self-expression. Over the centuries it has fueled such atrocities as inquisitions, witch hunts, abortion clinic bombings, "Red Scares," and the wholesale slaughter of Muslims, Christians, Hindus, and Jews. It goes without saying that the person who truly be-

---

*All biblical quotations are from the King James Version unless otherwise noted.

lieves in God has no need to perform such acts. Those who commit them are engaged in the work of *trying* to believe, not the work of belief itself.

God is forever giving us salvation for free (that is the lesson of the garden), but we won't take anything we can't pay for. Secretly, what we want most is control. We want to see where we are going. And if we're going to fall, we want to know where we are going to land. Because at bottom what we believe in most deeply and profoundly is ourselves. We don't understand that the thing we most believe in is a lie. This was the teaching offered by the Pure Land masters for nearly two thousand years, and, as I later came to realize, the core teaching of the Bible as well.

When I left the church as a teenager I never expected to come back to the Bible again. I certainly never expected I'd *want* to come back—that, in fact, I would spend the greater portion of my days studying it and thinking about it until I could recite sizable portions of it by heart. Nevertheless, when I returned to the scriptures after years of spiritual exploration, I was shocked to discover in the Bible the spiritual blueprint that explained everything I had experienced over the course of my journey, that the entire Bible was just the story of the struggle between Self and Other Power, beginning in its opening chapters with the fall of man and ending with the dawn of a new heaven and a new earth in the Book of Revelation. Taken individually or collectively, what we human beings most want is a way of assuring our salvation, and we will go to almost any lengths to achieve this on our own, as the Bible makes all too plain. But the one thing that will finally save us is beyond our power. That can only come from God.

A story from the Pure Land tradition illustrates this point.

About two hundred years ago in Japan there lived a holy man named Shoma. Unable to read or write, he had nevertheless cultivated a deep spiritual understanding. As a result people would come from miles around to seek his guidance about how to be reborn in the Pure Land, a heavenlike realm presided over by the savior Amida, the Buddha of Eternal Light and Life.

One day when Shoma had hired himself out as a laborer, a seeker arrived from several hundred miles away, having walked all that distance to ask Shoma what he should do to be saved. Shoma, who was pounding rice with a great wooden mallet at the time, just kept pounding without giving any indication that he had heard. The man asked again, but Shoma still would not look at him. When the people who had hired Shoma saw this, they felt pity for the man and begged Shoma to counsel him, but Shoma just kept on pounding rice. Finally, the visitor said in despair, "I've come such a long way, but if I can't learn how to be born in Amida's Pure Land, I have no choice but to return to my own village."

When he saw how miserable the man was, Shoma finally answered, "Why not ask Amida? He's the one who deals with such questions. It's really none of my business."

Simple as it is, I believe this story offers an important lesson about how to believe in God. "Why not ask Amida?" Those are not the words of a person who thinks of God in abstract terms, as an idea that needs to be tried or tested or intellectually understood. They are the words of one whose experience of salvation is fundamentally childlike, one whose experience of the divine is unmediated by any kind of intellectual filter. On the other hand, someone who travels hundreds of miles on foot, as Shoma's visitor did, cannot have done so without thinking of God as an idea. Otherwise, he would not have come. "If only the famous holy man Shoma will explain this idea to me," he thinks, "*then* I will be saved." But Shoma says, "Ask Amida. He's the one who answers questions like that."

Ours is the age of Self Power and, consequently, also the age of half-belief, an era when the very notion of the divine is undergoing the painful transition from personhood to idea, with the net result that people no longer know how to relate to it in a way that is simple, direct, and clear.

I said before that I didn't remember where along the way I'd lost my simplicity, but I remember exactly where I was when I found it again.

It was early one Saturday morning in the springtime, and as usual I was sitting in my rocking chair, the sole physical relic of my southern upbringing. I had long since given up the practice of meditating on a cushion on the floor. For several years, I'd been coming downstairs early each morning and fingering my old monk's beads for an hour or more while rocking and looking out at the backyard.

Maybe that morning it was the gentle rhythm of the rocker that helped put me in the right frame of mind, or maybe it was the Pure Land mantra I'd been reciting off and on for several years, which, after all, had much in common with the simple bedtime prayer I'd said as a child. There is no way to know for sure, and really, it doesn't matter. All I can say is that at some point the beginning and the end of my spiritual journey were brought together in a circle and tied off just like a string of beads, and for the first time in more than thirty years I felt the embrace of God, as surely as though he'd taken me up and held me upon his lap. And instantly I had the thought that no one could make this happen, as I'd tried for so long to do, and that there was likewise nothing anyone could do to take it away again. God was there for the having the moment we believed, and believing involved no preparation, no practice, and no calculation of any kind. Above all, it involved no delay. God was there already, always had been and always would be. To see him we only had to believe.

Naturally, there is no way anyone, myself included, can convince another person to do this—nor should we try. That work belongs to God, as the story of Shoma makes all too clear. Nevertheless, there is a place the Western spiritual seeker can turn for the inspiration to believe, and that place is just where it always has been: the Bible. Only first, we have to learn to read it for ourselves and not just to support the various norms and attitudes that make up a religion. We have to learn how to read it as a spiritual and not just a religious text.

It is a common argument among intellectuals today that human beings created God, rather than the other way around. But I do not believe that is so. That human beings created religion, however, I will gladly concede. And in the process they wrote the Bible. But in doing so, sometimes deliberately and sometimes in spite of themselves, they created more than a religion. They created the first great Western handbook on how to believe in God.

Belief

1

In the Beginning

And the earth was without form, and void;

and darkness was upon the face of the deep.

—GENESIS 1:2

Imagine a single bubble suddenly coming into consciousness of itself floating on the limitless vastness of a midnight sea. Surrounded by darkness on every side, it hangs atop the water in a weightless, directionless universe where it is not possible to say anything for sure. Whatever knowledge it can grasp hold of is only that of a sand grain, or of an atom—the kind of awareness that comes of recognizing oneself as impossibly insignificant and small.

The Bible opens with an image of roiling waters as far as the eye can see. There is no pole star, no reference point, no way of knowing where we are. At the beginning of the Bible we are lost. We are "in the dark" and "at sea."

If we look deep within ourselves, down to the core of our being, we can find that same awareness where it has lain undisturbed since the very first moment of Creation, untouched by the various certainties we use to console ourselves at any given moment—that we are safe and secure, or blameless, or correct in our religious or philosophical beliefs. The Bible begins with that awareness laid bare, inviting us to gaze into the deep, unfathomable waters that lie right below the surface of life.

What are those waters, and why does the Bible begin with them? This goes well beyond what we ordinarily think of as the big questions about life: Who am I? Who is God? Why am I here? To address these questions is itself to know the answer to the other three, because once we can understand the beginning of a thing, we can also know its middle and its end.

There is an episode from the Gospels that must always have been intended as a kind of commentary on that first primordial question.

Once when Jesus' disciples were crossing the Sea of Galilee, a great wind came up and tossed their ship upon the waves. Soon after, Jesus came walking to them across the sea. Thinking he might be some spirit come to destroy them, the disciples were afraid. "Lord, if it be thou, bid me come unto thee on the water," said Peter (Matthew 14:28), whereupon Jesus beckoned him out of the boat.

> And when Peter was come down out of the ship, he walked on the water, to go to Jesus. But when he saw the wind boisterous, he was afraid; and beginning to sink, he cried, saying, Lord, save me. And immediately Jesus stretched forth his hand, and caught him, and said unto him, O thou of little faith, wherefore didst thou doubt?
> (MATTHEW 14:29–31)

Some symbols are so primal, so close to the things they describe, we do better not to think of them as symbols at all, but simply take them as they are. What are the first waters of creation? Why, they are the very same waters that Jesus walks on in the Gospel of Matthew. The creation of dry land by God on the third day does nothing to assuage them. Those waters are always, always there. We each know this instinctively, with a knowledge that goes deeper than deep. It's not that those waters form the basic ground of our being; they are *below* the ground. They are what the ground is lying on. Were the ground we stand on ever to give way, that is where we would fall.

Beneath the seemingly solid foundations we establish for our lives—and these can be anything from a career to a relationship to an entire belief system, even a scientific or a religious one—there lies the spiritual void of a world without light or meaning. It is a place we all wish to avoid in this life, and we will go to any lengths to do so. We will distract ourselves with every imaginable form of entertainment, study theology, write dissertations, fight wars, and believe in almost anything, even if it is wrong. In extreme cases, we will even die to protect ourselves from this eventuality. In fact, we will do anything except what Jesus does—stand directly atop the chaos, with nothing between ourselves and the water but the belief that the universe will bear us up.

What does Jesus believe in? Or Moses? Or Adam or Abraham? They would say God. But what does that mean, really? Is belief in God like any other belief we use as a stopgap against existential anxiety? Is it merely something we put between ourselves and the water—like a dike or a boat? Realistically, this may be the case for many people, but it is not what the Bible means by belief. Belief is never a protection against life.

The Bible never really tells us where we are in the cosmos. It speaks in generic terms, as if orienting us within a room. But where is that room? We don't know. We have only its four walls, its ceiling and floor, and the various things, ourselves included, to be found within it. Here is the land, here the sky. The sun to mark the days, the moon for months, and stars for eternity. There are plants, animals, and others of our kind, and above it all stretches blue sky in all directions like the open hand of God. That hand matches the earth like the lid of a box. But what that box lies on is unknowable and unknown. Apart from belief there is no basis for life in this or any other world.

For thousands of years, the Bible's story of creation served as spiritual midwife for Western people. True, it asked us to believe in propositions for which there was no proof. But it was not asking us to believe for any ideological purpose. A particular church or religious institution might have a stake in whether or not its members believe in the literal truth of Creation, but the Bible has no such vested interest. It only wants us to realize that woven into the fabric of the universe itself is a spiritual buoyancy that allows us to tolerate the uncertainty of life in this world. What is being "created" in Genesis is not so much the physical universe as our belief in the rightness of that universe as a place to live and to be. All other interpretations, including those of the folklorist, the literalist, and the scientist, are finally beside the point.

To understand where a thing begins is to know where it is going and where it will end. Creation begins with chaos—with the uncertainty and unknowability that underlie all created things. From this God calls forth the perceptible order of a known universe, what today we would call reality. But where does the story end? "And God blessed the seventh day, and sanctified it: because that in it he had rested from all his work which God created and made" (Genesis 2:3). We may sometimes ask a person who is telling a roundabout story, "Where are you going with this?" If we ask the same question of the Bible—if we ask, "Where are you going with this creation story?"—the answer can only be the *Sabbath*, the seventh day of creation, on which God makes nothing but rest.

To be at rest in this world—and not to be in too great a hurry to get out of it, or to deny it, or control it, but to trust in it even as we trust in God—that is the point of the story of creation. Nothing more, nothing less. And rest has everything to do with belief. But not with the multiplicity of particular beliefs that make up a creed or dogma, a theology, a philosophy, or a religion. True rest lies in the single belief we call God, the belief that bears up the world we stand on, that allows us to live and act as conscious beings in the knowledge that, come what may, life in the world is essentially right and good. "And God saw that it was good," says the opening chapter of Genesis (1:10). Then, in case there should be any doubt on this matter, it says it again—seven times in all.

Before Josephine Slater came to live with my family in 1937, she had worked on my grandfather's farm in rural Arkansas. My mother had just been born and my grandmother needed someone to help out around the house, so my grandfather asked if Josephine would like to come work for him in town.

In preparation for her arrival, my grandfather built a small two-room house at the back of the property, connected to the main household by a narrow concrete walkway that bordered an enormous walnut tree. By the time I was born the roots had buckled the concrete so badly that as I was learning to walk I frequently had to be helped up over the hump. Eventually, however, I was able to negotiate the distance to Josephine's house on my own and, on days when my mother or grandmother lost track of my whereabouts in the house, I would invariably be found sitting on Josephine's lap on her front porch or curled up beside her on her bed.

It is always difficult to describe true believers. The problem is that the very things that distinguish them from others are easy to overlook: humility, quietness, a sense of inner calm. Many years later, describing the turmoil of his early childhood, my uncle would claim that it was really Josephine who kept the family from flying to pieces following my grandfather's premature death. "It was her patience more than anything, her stillness in the midst of everything that was wrong."

Josephine would do everything at exactly the same pace, regardless of what it was. It was as if she had made a pact with life to value all things in it as equal, giving the same attention to the postman and the pots and pans. I never learned the trick of it, if there was one, but I have finally come up with an image to describe what it felt like to observe her moving through the day. It was like watching the waves come in, one after another, to the shore.

In the afternoons I would often sit playing on the floor with a Duncan top or some other trinket from the drawer in the kitchen where she kept my toys. She would sit on the kitchen stool, watching me calmly without saying anything, and without picking up the newspaper or amusing herself in some other way. Whenever I looked up she would simply be looking back at me, as if to sit there looking were enough.

In the evenings we would relax together on one of the big white porch swings that faced one another across the expanse of my grandmother's deep covered porch. I remember sitting there beside her in my pajamas, listening to the chains of the swing squeak softly back and forth, just watching the darkness come.

One summer when I was three or four years old, I was sitting on Josephine's lap in her house in the late afternoon. She had not yet lit the kerosene reading lamp that sat on the table beside her bed. The sun shone through the back window and across the bedspread, casting a pattern of oblong leaf shadows across the wooden floor. It was hot. As we sat there together without saying anything, to cool our faces Josephine turned the handle of a cardboard fan very slowly back and forth across her wrist.

Oddly enough, the fan is what I remember. It was of a variety they handed out at hardware stores at Christmas every year—white fans with a color portrait of Jesus on one side, and on the other a calendar of the year. It has been a long time since I saw one like it, but I'm sure that somewhere down south they probably still exist.

In any case, it wasn't the fan that was important, but the slowness with which she turned it from side to side, without words or explanation, possibly without intention. Slipping back and forth across the space before us, it revealed first one face, and then the other—the temporal and the divine.

Finally, we can believe in God, even if we don't know who or what that is. Life is mysterious, uncertain, and occasionally terrifying, but there is no need to be dismayed. Walk or float, swim or tread water as we like, we only need to know this: the very thing that frightens us is the thing that holds us up.

2

The Knowledge of Good and Evil

But of the tree of the knowledge of good and evil,
thou shalt not eat of it: for in the day that thou
eatest thereof thou shalt surely die.

—GENESIS 2:17

Try, if you can, to get through one day without calling anything "bad." Try to remain open to the possibility that everything you see is acceptable (even optimal) as it is. If that is too hard, try for one day not to reject outright any person, place, or thing. This doesn't mean you become blind to reality. If you witness a crime, call the police. But leave judgment to God. God alone knows how all of creation fits together as a whole.

We live in a world defined by preferences—a world that sets one thing over and against another. If we are happy it is because we are not sad; if sad, because we are not happy. We experience success or failure, love or hate, attraction or revulsion. Rarely does it occur to us that there is another way, a way that accepts all created things, ourselves included, simply as they are. And yet, that other way exists. It begins at the moment we acknowledge that we are blinded by preference. We love our children and fear our enemies. Sometimes we hate them and seek their harm. To admit that is the first step toward recognizing a truth that lies at the heart of the truly religious life: *that which we cannot call good is the subject of all our spiritual work.*

We don't have to look far to find that kind of work. It presents itself in nearly every moment of our lives. "And God saw every thing that he had made, and, behold, it was very good" (Genesis 1:31). To grasp even the smallest portion of that truth may be the work of a lifetime.

Begin by looking in a mirror. What do you see? Few of us would say, "God." And yet the Bible boldly makes that claim: we are made in the image of the divine. But then why can't we see it? Why, when we look in the mirror, is it impossible to see God?

The difference between what we see and what we truly are is the product of our own thoughts and deeds. We are made in the image of the creator, but through acts of self-assertion we finally come to resemble no one but ourselves. No wonder when we look at our faces, we don't see any semblance of God. And yet it is there, beneath the worry lines and the makeup, behind the glasses or the beard. For it is not possible that once we have been created in God's image, that image should ever disappear. When our images of ourselves have all faded (as inevitably they must), God's image alone will remain. "For now we see through a glass, darkly," says Paul, "but then face to face: now I know in part; but then shall I know even as also I am known" (1 Corinthians 13:12).

But in that case, there is an obvious question: why breathe the eternal into the transitory, the divine spirit into mere earth and clay? "And the Lord God formed man of the dust of the ground, and breathed into his nostrils the breath of life; and man became a living soul" (Genesis 2:7). It is as if God took the entire universe and set it atop the altar of a single daisy. A beautiful thought. And yet, as human beings, we have to wonder why God did not make us of stronger stuff. Presumably dust was not the only option. Had he wanted, could he not have made us like the angels? Or is it that we were always meant to break?

The secret of true happiness lies in knowing that God does not make mistakes. God makes Adam from the dust of the ground because to make him from dust is perfect. Think of it. How could there have been a mistake in the creation? Are black holes a mistake? Is it a mistake that some squirrels are gray and some are brown? Or that the sky is blue? Is death a mistake? If so, then it is a mistake for everything in the universe, since all of it—even its stars—must eventually perish. It is only our self-centeredness that keeps us from applying that same logic to ourselves.

Really, it is this idea that there are mistakes—that certain things happen to us that ought not to, or ought to happen to somebody else, or ought not to happen to anyone—that is the source of all of our unhappiness as human beings. The moment we understand that God made no mistakes of creation is the moment we truly become free.

So why doesn't this happen? The answer is there at the beginning, in the opening chapters of the Bible.

God offers one and only one directive for life in Eden. The man and woman are told not to eat from the tree at the center of the garden, the tree of the knowledge of good and evil. And they are told why: "For in the day that thou eatest thereof thou shalt surely die" (Genesis 2:17).

It is wise not to interpret what transpires in Eden as merely historical. In that case it is not a very useful story. If original sin was something committed long ago by the first man and woman, then it can never be addressed—it happened, it's over, there is nothing we can do about it now. But that is not the case. The sin of the first man and woman is "original" because even now, at this very moment, it forms the basis of everything we think and do. The self, that seemingly indestructible shell that surrounds and imprisons the "living soul" within us, is composed entirely of our knowledge of good and evil. In the end it all comes down to this: we believe in a world with ourselves at the center, instead of the world created by God.

The moment Adam and Eve eat from the tree of knowledge, they find themselves alone in a world reinterpreted entirely from their own limited point of view. What is good is good for the self—and likewise, what is evil. And what is the greatest evil from their point of view? Death—just as God had warned. Death, as much a part of man as the dust from which he is made, is nevertheless, from the standpoint of the individual self, the ultimate insult, just as the ultimate good becomes a life without limit or restriction—a life in which the self can protect and extend its influence indefinitely, and assert its will however it might please. And so it goes . . . Can it be any wonder that the rest of the Bible is so filled with heartbreak, loss, misunderstanding, even murder? Once humankind has taken on the knowledge of good and evil, there is no other way that events can transpire. From time to time God intervenes to forgive or rebuke, and—more often than not—to deliver them, but the truth is, what they need to be delivered from is themselves. That is the problem. Good and evil are too much for them. That knowledge belongs to God, who alone, in all the universe, is vast enough to contain and to reconcile it.

As she lay on the verge of death, the medieval mystic Julian of Norwich suffered in anguish over the inescapability of sin. She thought back on the story of Eden and wondered, "If sin had not been, we should all have been clean and like to our Lord, as He made us." But Jesus appeared to her in a vision and said, "It is true that sin is the cause of all this pain; but all shall be well, and all shall be well, and all manner of thing shall be well."

"This was said full tenderly, showing no manner of blame to me nor anyone else," writes Julian. "And in these words I saw a marvelous high mystery hid in God." And Julian awoke, and survived, and found the world reborn.

Julian lived in fourteenth-century England, at a time when suffering and brutality practically defined human life. Mothers died in childbirth, often as not their children died too, and hunger and disease (including the plague) were facts of daily life. War was common, and justice (when and where it was available) was meted out selectively and with a violence we can scarcely imagine today. Through it all Julian lived in an anchorage attached to Norwich Cathedral, a kind of semiprivate dwelling that, although she never left it until the day she died, nevertheless afforded her constant contact with the people of the town, who frequently visited her to ask her for prayers, to seek spiritual guidance, and increasingly to seek her advice on how to live. These were the people to whom she offered her message of radical grace: "And all shall be well, and all shall be well, and all manner of thing shall be well."

Shocking as it may seem from a conventional moral point of view, it is not possible to know God, or even truly to believe in him, and also believe in good and evil. Good and evil belong to the self, not the soul. And, sadly, the self belongs to them. This is the source of all of our pain and suffering as human beings and, as Jesus suggested to Julian, it truly is the original sin—the cause of all our pain. "And all shall be well, and all shall be well, and all manner of thing shall be well." But we don't believe it. We'd rather take the fruit.

3

Cain and Abel

And Abel, he also brought of the firstlings of his flock and
of the fat thereof. And the Lord had respect unto Abel and to his
offering: But unto Cain and to his offering he had not respect.

—GENESIS 4:4–5

Despite the fact that he is remembered as the first murderer, it is Cain, not Abel, who draws most people's sympathy when they think of the story of the first brothers. Why did God reject his offering? Was it simply the luck of the draw?

Cain made his offering first, giving his younger brother the opportunity to best him. Going out to the pasture, Abel then took the choicest portion of his livestock and brought it before the Lord. We can imagine Cain, even before the outcome was clear, anxiously waiting to see how it would go. Then the decision: "And the Lord had respect unto Abel and to his offering: But unto Cain and his offering he had not respect" (Genesis 4:4–5).

What did Cain do wrong? Abel brought the firstborn of his flock as his offering, Cain the fruit of the ground. Does God prefer a blood sacrifice over a grain offering, or is it the inner process he observes: the fact that Abel seems to have deliberated over the choice, bringing the finest animals from his flock? At this point it is impossible to tell. The simple truth is, we make mistakes—all the time. In every moment, just by being alive, we act, and every action, even the smallest, most inconsequential action, has unforeseeable consequences, like a pebble tossed into a pool. Who knows how far the ripples will go or what their effect will be? The whole notion of doing everything right is possible only if we define "right" very narrowly, in terms of what has a foreseeably good outcome for ourselves, for those we know, or perhaps for our species or our "tribe." And even then . . . well, we really just don't know. Automobiles seemed like a good idea at one time; now global warming does not. What's more important is how we respond to mistakes once they become apparent. That is the point of the story.

When his offering is rejected, Cain seems angry and depressed. "Why art thou wroth? and why is thy countenance fallen?" God asks him. "If thou doest well, shalt thou not be accepted?" (Genesis 4:6–7). If it is God's sympathy Cain expects, he doesn't get it. What God has in mind for his first grandson at this moment in the story is something far better than sympathy. Better than respect even. For the gift he offers is a teaching on how to avoid this kind of suffering altogether. It is, quite simply, a way out of the whole game. This is how it always happens in the Bible. The openings come when we least expect them, or deserve them—and usually in times of crisis. Oddly enough, those seem to be the moments when we are most susceptible to God.

"If thou doest well, shalt thou not be accepted?" God tells Cain. But what does he mean by "doing well"? Is it about the offering again? I think not. In that case, there would be no lesson, only a specific injunction— "You should have done this, not that." No. It is more than that. What God is talking about is bigger than the rejected offering. It's all about Cain's *re-action* to it. In fact, that is the point of unfolding for the entire story.

If life teaches us one lesson, it is that it is often unpredictable. Consequently, no matter how hard we try, or how good we are at winning, inevitably sometimes we will lose. When that happens, some people blame God, while others blame themselves, and still others, like Cain, blame someone else. But an event is simply an event. To win approval is one kind of event. To lose it is another. To be invested in the outcome of events is forever to be trapped in the idea of gain and loss. And in that case there can be no peace, either in the inner or the outer world. There will always be some kind of war.

When God says "If thou doest well . . ." he points toward an entirely different way of being than the one Cain finds himself stuck in at that moment in the story—a way that transcends opposites of all kinds: gain and loss, approval and non-approval, good and evil, birth and death. And what is that way? What does it mean "to do well"?

To do well means to allow ourselves the possibility of a fresh beginning with each new moment of life. In a word, it means *freedom*— freedom from shame, freedom from blame, freedom from the endless mistakes we make simply by virtue of being alive. That freedom comes to us in every second, with every heartbeat and every breath. And yet, how hard it is to let go of our accumulated resentments, heartaches, and disappointments. All too often, it seems, we would rather be unhappy instead.

"And if thou doest *not* well," warns God, "sin lieth at the door" (Genesis 4:7). A certain type of theology likes to insist that man's nature is inherently sinful. But here God seems to tell us that the choice is ours. It's like crossing a threshold, he says. On one side is eternity, on the other sin and death. Like his parents before him, Cain crosses that threshold, choosing the knowledge of good and evil and all that accompanies it, and rather than mastering sin, is mastered by it. First he becomes its victim. And then he makes a victim of his brother. For the two always go hand in hand. Once we have chosen the knowledge of good and evil, there will always be some kind of war.

And what of the rest of the story? We are told that after the murder Cain was banished from the presence of God and sent off east of Eden to dwell in the land of Nod. There he met a girl, presumably from some other Middle Eastern creation story, and together they had a son, Enoch, after whom Cain named the first city. Of Cain's death we are told nothing, and of his spiritual life not one word more.

And yet I think it would be deluded to assume that Cain is doomed. For all that could change in an instant, because the land of Nod is not so far from Eden as we think.

4

The Unfinished Tower

And the Lord said, Behold, the people is one, and they have all
one language; and this they begin to do: and now nothing will be
restrained from them, which they have imagined to do.

—GENESIS 11:6

According to Genesis, the survivors of the flood were originally one people of one language who decided to make a name for themselves by
building a tower that reached into the heavens. But when God saw what
they were about, he confused their speech, and scattered them across the
face of the earth—and the tower remained unfinished.

How could it be wrong for the whole world to be of one mind and of
one speech? Isn't the multiplicity of languages, cultures, and beliefs the
great source of misunderstanding among the various peoples of the
world? Don't we all secretly prefer friends who think and speak as we do,
who eat the same food, read the same novels, watch the same sporting
events, and share the same opinions? Doesn't it make us uncomfortable
to spend time with people whose way of life is very different from our
own? In short, wouldn't it be better if we were all the same? Maybe not.

For history has shown us through many examples, from the Inquisition to the rise of fascism, what happens when a single notion of good and evil prevails.

Babel is usually interpreted as a story about the folly of human pride. In reality, however, the driving force behind the tower is not pride, but insecurity. The impulse to create one people—of one culture, one language, and one religion—can arise from nothing else. Think about it. What drives us to convert our neighbor to our way of thinking? Is it really just political or religious concerns that motivate us? Isn't it really just the answer to a very simple, universal need: to feel grounded in our moral and religious beliefs, to feel the earth as solid beneath our feet?

Sadly, the earth is not solid, and never has been—not from the very dawn of time. Apart from belief there is no basis for life in this or any other world. Apart from belief there is no place to stand. Belief is primary. Belief is fundamental. And each and every one of us is responsible for what we stand on. We are responsible for what we believe, and this fact is terrifying. The more people sign on to our particular system of belief—whether it is a social, a religious, or a scientific one—the safer we feel. The more people embrace it, the more faith we have in ourselves as the ultimate arbiters of right and wrong—which is to say, the more faith we have in our "self." Naturally, those people whose beliefs are different may pose a challenge to that system and that self, in which case either we must convert them, or we must prove them wrong. In extreme cases, we may even need to destroy them to protect what we believe. Clearly, the collective beliefs of such a "belief system" are not the same as belief in God. In fact, they are antithetical to true belief.

God understands that the people of Babel are building more than just a tower. The tower is only a symbol. Therefore he does nothing to topple it, which presumably he could. Instead, he strikes at the heart of the problem, confounding the language of the people so that they can no longer encourage one another in their collective delusion. He scatters them over the face of the earth, providing the occasion for a multiplicity of cultures and beliefs, because only in that way can he protect them from themselves.

We can believe in the self or we can believe in God, but we cannot believe in both. Of course, we all experience the self as a reality. Each of us has a name, a personal history, a unique set of relationships to other people and to the world. But for that very reason there is no need to believe in it. The self is just a fact. It doesn't really warrant the power of belief. It is not necessary to believe in it because we experience it directly. Not so with God.

God lies beyond fact and fiction in a realm that surpasses all we could ever hope to comprehend. God is beyond our frame of reference, beyond the frame of reality itself as the origin and ultimate destination of all things. Our only access to him is through belief. If we believe in him, we see him. If not, then we don't. Usually we say that seeing is believing. But it is unwise to apply that worldly logic to matters of the spirit or the heart. To understand the truths of the spirit, we must come to understand that just the opposite is true: believing is seeing. We cannot see any sign of God's presence in the world before we believe.

During the mid-1970s, while attending college in rural Tennessee, I had the privilege of knowing a Chinese Zen master who embodied God's presence more than anyone I have ever met, though I didn't recognize it at the time. I'd just returned from a year off, during which I'd studied at a Japanese-style Buddhist monastery in upstate New York, where I developed rather inflexible expectations about what a Zen master ought to look and act like. Consequently, everything about Deh Chun threw me off.

The day after my return to the university, my art history professor, hearing that I'd been off studying Zen for the year, casually remarked that there was a Ch'an (Chinese Zen) master living happily, of all places, amid the local rednecks at the end of a chained-dog road in nearby Monteagle. He was an eccentric, she warned, but quite possibly one of the finest traditional landscape painters to have survived the Cultural Revolution.

I arrived at Deh Chun's little two-room shack behind the Dairy Queen to find him even smaller and frailer looking than I could have expected, dressed in Salvation Army–issue slacks and sports coat, with a very short gray stubble covering both his chin and his head. If he had monks' robes I never saw him wear them. For that matter, only once thereafter, when I invited him to dinner to meet my religion professor, did I ever see him wear his teeth. There was nothing whatsoever imposing about his manner or appearance. In fact, at first I couldn't be sure whether my difficulty in communicating exactly why I had come to see him had to do with his poor command of English or whether he was somewhat mentally challenged—or, given his age, maybe senile.

Now I wonder if maybe I wasn't the mentally challenged one after all. At twenty, I was able to recognize in Deh Chun something I couldn't put a name to. I was fairly certain he'd had the same kind of spiritual breakthrough I'd experienced the year before, but since he never spoke of such matters with me and steadfastly refused to say anything about Buddhism, I assumed he had nothing to teach. He would invite me to have lunch or breakfast with him instead, or to work in his garden, or take a drive through the mountains, or just sit quietly drinking tea by the wood stove in his dim, unlit house, not saying anything in particular for minutes or hours on end.

And that is probably why I chose to study formally with the Japanese Zen master I'd met the year before instead—because Deh Chun hadn't worn a golden robe, didn't line up his students in a row for morning meditation, and never once in my hearing spoke of Buddhism as the best or the only way. Because he never taught me anything beyond the simplest truths of life, like sharing food and love and work. Because in all the time I knew him he offered not one excuse for giving up my simplicity, for thinking of myself as special, or for putting Buddhism, or anything else for that matter, between myself and God. Deh Chun's religion was so simple it was invisible—like it wasn't there at all. Only many years later, as I was poised to assume the formal duties of a Zen master, did it occur to me that I had missed something vital about Deh Chun, that without making a big deal about it or calling attention to it in any way, he had given me a glimpse at true religious belief—after which it was impossible to go on building the Zen tower I'd kept myself busy with for so many years.

Belief is the spy hole through which we see into another world. It may be a very small opening, but even that is enough. That world has been called by various names in different cultures: heaven, the Pure Land, the Elysian Fields, or the kingdom of God. But we have no access to that world apart from belief. "For we walk by faith, not by sight" (2 Corinthians 5:7), says Paul. Finally, we must simply open our hearts and believe.

The story of Babel is all about the loss of this individual experience of God. That is why at the end of the story God says to his angels: "Go to, let us go down, and there confound their language, that they may not understand one another's speech" (Genesis 11:7). God doesn't want one people, of one language and one mind, who trade on their collective might for a sense of purpose and meaning in the world. He has no desire for a monolithic culture convinced of the infallibility of its own moral vision. He wants a relationship with each individual in the most optimal and unique possible way. But in order for that to happen, we must be ready to believe for ourselves.

A Hindu fable, also recounted by the Buddha, tells the story of a wise Raja who once commanded that all the blind men of his kingdom be gathered together. When they were all assembled, he had an elephant brought into their midst. Guiding them up to the beast, he laid the hands of one upon the tusk, the hands of another upon the tail, and likewise with the trunk, the foot, the belly, and all other parts of the animal.

"This is an elephant," he told them. "Now tell me what you think of it."

And so each blind man began to offer his opinion. The one who had touched the tusk said, "An elephant is like a plowshare." The one who had touched the tail said, "No, an elephant is just like a whisk for brushing away flies." The one who had touched the leg said, "No, it's not that either; it is exactly like a tree." And so forth and so on. One by one, each blind man offered an opinion based on the part of the animal he had touched. But the Raja only laughed.

Each of us is a blind man touching an elephant where God is concerned. And this is as it should be. However convinced we may feel of the rightness of our moral or theological vision, we never touch more than the smallest part of God. But this is not a problem so long as we remain humble and open. It is not a problem so long as we allow ourselves to be informed by other points of view.

That is why Jesus once remarked to his disciples, "For where two or three are gathered together in my name, there am I in the midst of them" (Matthew 18:20). When Christians read those words today they are apt to interpret them as a call to church or some other form of Christian fellowship. But I tend to think that if Jesus were here today he would think of such a gathering as including Jews and Muslims, and just possibly a Chinese Buddhist hermit to make everyone breakfast or a cup of tea.

5

Going Forth

Now the Lord had said unto Abram, Get thee out of thy country,

and from thy kindred, and from thy father's house,

unto a land that I will shew thee.

—GENESIS 12:1

The Bible says nothing of the life of Abram, the founder of Western monotheism, before the moment God says to him, *lech-lecha*: "Go forth!" A Jewish legend, however, also repeated in the Qur'an, tells us that his father, Terah, was a prosperous idol maker who carved the wooden gods worshipped by the people of his native city of Haran.

According to the story, one afternoon when Terah was away, the young Abram took an ax and smashed every idol in his father's shop save one. Then, tying the ax to the god's hand with a piece of cord, he waited calmly for his father's return.

When Terah saw the destruction, he immediately accused Abram, but Abram only pointed at the remaining god and claimed, "That big one grew angry with the others and dashed them all to bits."

This made Terah more incensed than ever. "These gods are made of wood!" he cried. "They aren't capable of movement or action." Whereupon Abram said to his father, "Shouldn't your ears listen to what your own mouth is saying?"

What does it mean to leave our country, our family, and our parents' house? Doesn't it mean giving up all of our idols, all the sources of safety and identity that serve as outward and inward signs of belonging, making our lives feel solid and predictable? Doesn't it really mean to leave the security of the tribe?

Few of us today think of ourselves as belonging to a "tribe." The word calls to mind a more primitive era in which people lived in smaller, more homogenous social groups. But human nature has changed very little in four thousand years, and our identities are no less tribal today than they were before.

What defines a tribe is a set of beliefs interpreted as facts. We may believe that it is all right to be homosexual, or we may believe that homosexuality is a sin. We may believe in what can be proven by science, or that scripture is the final authority about the world. We may belong to the tribe of those who believe in God, or the tribe of those who do not. But if we interpret any of those beliefs in such a way that they separate us from others, then we have taken a step away from belief itself, which always seizes us from within, hand in glove, revealing our common humanity first and last of all. The point of life is to journey *toward* that subjective, purely human kind of belief, not away from it. But to do that we must make a rather peculiar kind of journey, the destination of which necessarily always lies within.

The story of Abraham, as he later comes to be known, is a way of showing us, in outward, dramatic terms, how that inward journey takes place. God speaks to Abraham (how we are not told), and tells him that he will bless him and make him a great nation, but that he must leave behind all he knows and travel to a land that God will show him. It is always like this—heaven, Canaan, the Promised Land. We always begin by leaving the world we know—the one we can see, hear, smell, taste, and touch—in search of a world we cannot imagine. Paul says that we walk by faith, not by sight; and St. John of the Cross teaches that we must pass through the "dark night of the soul" in order to reach God. Both are just ways of saying that it is impossible to complete the journey of belief without leaving what we know.

The spiritual journey makes no sense from that ordinary mind-set by which we habitually do everything in our power to solidify and defend our point of view. God says to Abraham, "Leave all of that behind you." It only stands to reason that what Abraham is being sent *to* is not simply more of the same—more powerless idols, more self-centeredness, more of the same socially conditioned consciousness, only dressed up in a slightly different way. He is being asked to found a religion, but a religion is not just another tribal identity, not just the self dressed up in disguise. Whatever becomes of it in the end, in the beginning it is always more than that. We may end up a priest or rabbi, but it is always as an Abraham that the spiritual journey begins.

A similar journey takes place at the beginning of the New Testament, only in this case the journey is not an outward one—the distance traveled is only that between the head and the heart.

The Gospel of Matthew opens with a genealogy testifying to the fact that Jesus is descended from Abraham. But in the last entry in that genealogy it becomes clear that, in the biological sense at least, Jesus may not be descended from Abraham at all, not through Joseph at any rate: "And Jacob begat Joseph the husband of Mary, of whom was born Jesus, who is called Christ" (Matthew 1:16). "Of whom was born . . ." According to the Bible, Jesus is not the son of Joseph, but of Mary, who has become pregnant while she is betrothed to Joseph, inviting at best a scandal, at worst death by stoning. It is only because Joseph seems willing to divorce her quietly that disaster is averted. Even so, the child seems destined to be born out of wedlock and therefore not in a position to fulfill his destiny in the world. Indeed, a few verses later, when Joseph is considering what to do, he has a dream in which he is told by an angel, "Fear not to take unto thee Mary thy wife: for that which is conceived in her is of the Holy Ghost" (Matthew 1:20).

God speaks to us in dreams and in quiet waking moments as if from the bottomless well of our being, a voice that rises clear and distinct from the center, like the sound of pure life-giving water. Sometimes we drop a stone into that well and wait to hear a sound from the depths below. This we call prayer. That is what Joseph does when he falls asleep thinking of what to do about Mary, not praying in a self-conscious way perhaps, but in the manner of a man faced with a seemingly unsolvable problem who wrestles with it late into the night.

There is no problem from a tribal point of view. Joseph can bow to the letter of Jewish law and consider himself a good person in the eyes of the society in which he lives: "Then they shall bring out the damsel to the door of her father's house, and the men of her city shall stone her with stones that she die: because she hath wrought folly in Israel, to play the whore in her father's house: so shalt thou put evil away from among you" (Deuteronomy 22:21). But of course Joseph can't bring himself to do this. He finds it difficult to consider even the accepted custom of preemptively divorcing her. Perhaps he loves Mary. We never know. We are told only about the dream and the angel. It is the Bible's way of telling us that a profound transformation has taken place, an inner revolution that allows Joseph to midwife the birth of mercy and salvation into the world.

We are not most of us spiritual pioneers. We do not live at the beginning of a great religious age, as Abraham did, or, like Joseph, in the middle of one, when tribal custom had largely replaced belief in God. We live in an age when traditional religious beliefs are colliding with such force that they threaten to destroy one another, either through violence itself or through the moral decline that virtually always adheres to those who commit such violence, ironically destroying from within the very spiritual impulse they sought to protect by attacking one another.

A new spiritual destiny lies before us as people living in a global age, and that destiny consists in choosing a God who loves all of humanity with equal passion—and all of nature besides—over the multiplicity of false gods we have created for selfish purposes, to protect our individual societies and ourselves. Like Abraham, we are being shown a new land. Like Joseph, we are being asked to midwife the birth of mercy and salvation into the world.

I have to admit that even though I hadn't been a Christian for many years by the time I discovered it, I was still shocked and, truth be told, a little brokenhearted to discover the truth of Jesus' patrimony. Tribal beliefs always die hard—especially the ones we grew up with as a child.

I'd always taken it for granted that Jesus was descended in a direct line through David, Ruth, and Jacob, all the way back to Abraham. Somehow it seemed an important part of Jesus' spiritual authority and the patrilinear logic of the Bible that the "seed of Jesse" had been carefully handed down. Even during my years as a Buddhist, when I no longer believed that Jesus was the son of God, somehow I still believed he was the son of David, as I'd heard read aloud in church every Christmas of my life. And yet the plain truth of it was there in the Bible for anyone to see. Jesus was Mary's son, not Joseph's. And Mary's lineage is nowhere listed in the Bible.

Although I don't know if the following version of events is any truer than the one I learned at Sunday school, there is a kind of spiritual logic to it that transcends the human attachment to lineages and other symbols of spiritual authority. According to one theory, Jesus' father may, in fact, have been a soldier stationed in Palestine as part of the occupying

Roman force, which would explain the horror that people felt at what must otherwise have been an all too common occurrence. It isn't a particularly inspiring explanation, but these days I almost prefer it over the one I grew up with, because it answers a question I always had, even as a child, about how Jesus could have been "conceived of the Holy Spirit," as is maintained both in the Bible and in the Apostle's Creed.

Not that Jesus couldn't have been conceived in some miraculous way. Who can say? In my years of spiritual seeking, I have witnessed things no one could explain. Nevertheless, if we allow the lesser supernatural miracle to displace the greater, wholly natural one, we have missed the point of the story. The real miracle, the real descent of the Holy Spirit, doesn't come just through Mary, but through Joseph as well, at the moment he resolves to set aside rumor, reputation, and the strictures of societal convention, and accept the child of his rival (and for all he knows, maybe the child of his Roman enemy) as his own. That is the true miracle of the story, the moment of "going forth," without which there is no journey toward a New Covenant of mercy and forgiveness, without which there is no Jesus even. Whatever seed the Holy Spirit may have sown in Mary's womb, it would never have grown were it not for Joseph.

Finally, it is not through Joseph's loins but through his heart that Jesus comes into the world. And in that transformation he is united, not just by blood, but by spirit, with a lineage stretching back clear to the boy who smashed his father's idols. It happens through an inner revolution of the heart that takes place at the moment he listens to the voice of the angel, shattering the selfishness of man-made religious proscriptions so that the seed of true spirit may grow. No wonder, when he is grown, Jesus thinks of God as a loving father. Consider the father he had.

6

The Binding of Isaac

And he said, Take now thy son, thine only son Isaac,

whom thou lovest, and get thee into the land of Moriah;

and offer him there for a burnt offering upon one

of the mountains which I will tell thee of.

—GENESIS 22:2

The Danish philosopher Søren Kierkegaard said about what is probably the most disturbing episode in all of Genesis, if not the entire Bible, "Though Abraham arouses my admiration, at the same time he appalls me."

Like nearly everyone else who has ever read the story of a father's willingness to sacrifice his son, Kierkegaard felt a mingling of astonishment that Abraham's faith could be so strong, and horror for the very same reason. Nevertheless, he recognized in the Binding of Isaac something that touched the knot of our common suffering in this world. "He who has explained this riddle," he confessed finally, "has explained my life."

When we drop the stone of prayer to the depths of our being, there is no telling what may call back out of those depths. God speaks to Abraham in the dead of night when all others are asleep, commanding him to sacrifice his son upon a mountain he will be guided to. Perhaps God's voice came to him in a dream; we never know. All we are told is that at dawn Abraham rose to carry out God's command, cutting wood for the fire and gathering his son Isaac and his two servants together for the journey. When Isaac asks, "Where is the lamb for the sacrifice?" Abraham replies only, "God will provide himself a lamb for a burnt offering" (Genesis 22:8).

The thought that God might provide a less grisly alternative (as indeed happens) does little to blunt our horror at such a response, because Abraham could just as easily be referring to Isaac himself. Isn't God's own son referred to as a "lamb" later in the Bible? And is that son not sacrificed in the end? There is little reason to hope for a positive outcome and, indeed, when the moment of truth finally arrives, Abraham shows himself fully willing to slay his own flesh and blood.

There is no way around this. As facts go in the Bible, Abraham's willingness to sacrifice his child has all the stubborn intransigence of a stone. We might insist that he knew all along God would intervene, if that helps us to tolerate what is otherwise unthinkable. But the truth is, there is no hesitation whatsoever in Abraham's actions. The angel himself, sent by God to witness the unfolding of the event, seems to understand this quite well. At the last possible moment, he cries, "Abraham! Abraham!" repeating the name to make sure that he has been heard. "Lay not thine hand upon the lad, neither do thou any thing unto him: for now I know that thou fearest God, seeing thou hast not withheld thy son, thine only son from me" (Genesis 22:11–12). And at that moment Abraham lifts his eyes and spies a ram with its horns caught in a thicket, and offers that instead of his son.

The only thing that makes the story tolerable for most people is the knowledge, offered in the very first line, that God was "tempting" Abraham by asking him to sacrifice his son. In other words, we know from the start what Abraham does not: the whole episode is just a test. But then, that poses a terrifying question: has Abraham passed—or failed? If by showing himself willing to sacrifice his son to God he has passed the test, could not the same be asked of us? And if he has failed for the same reason, proving himself supremely unworthy as a father and a husband, what chance do ordinary people with ordinary values have of ever finding favor with God?

The Binding of Isaac has long been interpreted as the ultimate example of faith. It seems to depict a man whose belief in God is so resolute that he is willing to sacrifice everything for the sake of it. But I do not believe that this is finally the point of the story. Belief is internal. It requires no outward show. You have it or you don't, and no amount of sacrifice, however dire or extreme or theatrically acted out, will alter that fact either way. We believe or we do not; it's always as simple as that.

But then, why must Abraham be tested? If God has really spoken to him and he is not just another of those overstressed, psychotic parents who hear voices telling them to kill their children, what is the point of telling him to sacrifice his son? If it is loyalty God expects from Abraham—*loyalty* being just another word for fidelity to the tribe—then it is an awful test, unworthy of any but the most ruthless, bloodthirsty God. If, on the other hand, it is Abraham's belief that is being tested, to show God—and presumably Abraham himself—where he stands, then we must read the story in a very different way. Then it becomes a story without any tribal implications whatsoever.

Earlier I wrote about the need for the singular belief in that which we call God, rather than the multiplicity of beliefs that compose a religious or cultural worldview. What is being tested in the story of Abraham and Isaac is whether or not Abraham possesses that singular transcendent belief or only its worldly counterfeit, full belief or only half. Finally, it seems that the former is true.

In the end, Abraham looks up to find the ram with its horns caught in a thicket and sacrifices that instead of his son. It is the moment of sanity we have all been hoping for, as disappointing as it might seem from a modern animal-rights point of view. The moment when Abraham shakes off the whole nightmarish event and realizes that what God has *asked* for is not what God *intends*—which is that Abraham's son may live, and his people be blessed. It is a moment of transcendence—quite literally a moment of "looking up."

Abraham's predicament, though the most extreme possible example, is nevertheless one we face all the time. At some point in any given day, we look up from that narrow place where our options have dwindled to almost none to find that, in our efforts to calculate the odds of life in our favor, we have left God out of the equation. That moment of looking up is at once a moment of remembering God and a moment of liberation, a moment when we remember that, whatever problem we may be facing, whatever tight spot we might currently be caught in, God is not the problem but the solution. In fact, God is *never* part of our problem. He never climbs with us into the narrow box of our conditioned way of thinking, but waits outside for the moment we remember him again. It is always a joyous moment. Even when the solution is only to relax and, as the expression says, "Let go and let God."

Until the moment in the story when Abraham spies the ram, he is almost an automaton. His lack of any emotion during the whole episode would seem to indicate that he is in the grip of an overpowering compulsion to act against his nature, that he is, in effect, like a ball caught in a groove. For this reason, some have suggested that the whole episode is a hearkening back to the days when people actually believed they *had* to offer human sacrifices to the gods in order to appease them, by which logic Abraham is well within his rights to kill Isaac, just as Joseph would have been justified by Jewish law in having Mary stoned. But of course Abraham doesn't want to kill his son any more than Joseph wants Mary to die, and he realizes at the last possible moment that God doesn't want that kind of sacrifice either.

What God *does* want is belief. But not for his own satisfaction. God wants belief because only belief in a Power Beyond the Self can make us look up, thereby freeing us to act in accordance with changing circumstances as they arise. What God wants, and human beings need, is the flexibility of belief that accompanies an ongoing relationship. That is why nowadays I like the motto of the United Church of Christ: "God is still speaking." In a world where God is still speaking, we look up to find a ram in the thicket. In a world where God is silent, it is only our own voices we hear, and Isaac always dies.

7

Jacob and the Angel

And Jacob was left alone; and there wrestled a man
with him until the breaking of the day.

—GENESIS 32:24

When we are young we can avoid our problems—or at least ignore them to some extent. As we grow older, however, there comes a moment (usually a moment of crisis) when they all come home to roost, a moment when we must wrestle with the issues that have followed us all of our lives and finally deal with them—or not. This is where we find Jacob on the night of his struggle with the angel.

Jacob is traveling back to his homeland, from which he has been in exile for twenty years. There he will have to confront his brother, Esau, who, having been deprived of their father's blessing by Jacob, has sworn to kill him. Earlier that day, a group of scouts returns to Jacob's camp to tell him that Esau himself is approaching with a retinue of four hundred men. Despite the fact that he has amassed great wealth during his exile in Haran, and therefore presumably has men of his own, Jacob is distraught. He is traveling with his wives and children.

That night Jacob offers a prayer to God that begins, "I am not worthy . . ." and concludes, "Deliver me, I pray thee, from the hand of my brother, from the hand of Esau: for I fear him, lest he will come and smite me, and the mother with the children" (Genesis 32:11). Afterward he sends his servants on ahead with gifts for Esau, then takes his family and all his livestock across the river, and returns to pass the night alone—or so he thinks.

The spiritual life always involves a struggle for belief. We sometimes say of those who are in the throes of some great difficulty that they are "wrestling with an addiction" or "struggling with a deep personal problem." Part of them says one thing, and part of them another. In its simplest form, wrestling for belief involves the struggle between that part of us that wants to believe and that part of us that cannot.

In Jacob's case the struggle is obvious. If he believed, he would have remained across the river with his family and his possessions. But he doesn't—not fully anyway—and so nightfall finds him back on the near bank again, unable to go forward with his life. The angel appears as a way of making this obvious. Jacob has to wrestle with him before he can go on.

In the struggle for belief, two forces are at work within us: faith and doubt. From the religious point of view, one might think faith ought to prevail; from the scientific rationalist view, that doubt (or healthy skepticism, at least) ought to reign. But each is necessary if belief is ever to become settled within us. If either force wins the upper hand in that struggle, the battle for belief is lost. Either we end up with a faith that must defend itself against the very doubts it claims to have vanquished (but in reality has only suppressed or projected onto others) or we find ourselves cut off at the spiritual root, left with a God-shaped hole that no scientific rationalism or secular humanism or power of myth will ever fill. In either case we fail to attain the one thing that would set our hearts at peace and provide the basis for real spiritual fulfillment in our lives.

Unfortunately, in the beginning at least, most of us don't wrestle for belief. When doubt appears, we either let go of faith immediately and walk away—into science, reason, indifference, or the purely secular life— or else we regard its appearance as a sign of spiritual weakness. If we are to have faith, we must be rid of doubt by whatever means, or so it seems, and that usually means simply pushing it away. Without doubt, however, the best we can attain is only half-belief.

The problem in most cases is not a lack of intellectual doubt, the kind of doubt favored by the nonbeliever, which tends to focus on what can or cannot be objectively demonstrated to be true. What is lacking is the *subjective,* emotionally connected doubt that there will be someone there to save us when we cannot save ourselves. That is what it means to "wrestle with God." It means to ask, very simply, but profoundly, "God, are you really there?" One must be courageous to ask such a question, for it exposes our vulnerability. Because once we ask that question we have already begun to fall.

Not long after the experience of thinking my plane was going down, I decided to begin reading the Bible again after a lapse of more than thirty years. All things considered, it seemed best to get reacquainted with my spiritual roots. It was a little like coming home after having lived for many decades in another country where they spoke a different language and lived by entirely different customs.

At first I felt some disorientation. The more I read, however, the more I discovered in the Bible the same spiritual teachings I'd found in Buddhism, only expressed in the language I'd grown up with. And the more I read the more convinced I became that it was *because* I had studied Buddhism that I was able to recognize those teachings for what they were. They'd been so distorted by the Christianity I'd grown up with that they were no longer recognizable without some other tradition to take my bearings from. But once that element was in place, it was like reading the Bible for the very first time.

A few months later, I posted flyers around Woodstock advertising a new kind of Bible study for which no religious background or affiliation was required. You simply had to bring your questions about God and the Bible and be willing to discuss them with others in an honest, open-minded way.

There is a well-known religious joke that asks, "What do you get when you cross a Jehovah's Witness with a Unitarian?" The answer is, "A man in a suit on your doorstep who has no idea why he is there." The humor here plays off the contrast between those whose religion tells them exactly what to believe and how to believe it, and those whose religion tells them nothing—or rather everything at once, which amounts to about the same thing.

Our Woodstock Bible study group was a little like that, although in our case the question might have been "What do you get when you cross an *ex*–Jehovah's Witness with an *ex*-Unitarian?" From the beginning, we attracted an amazingly diverse membership. There were practicing Jews and Christians (in roughly equal proportion), in addition to Buddhists, Sufis, and the followers of half a dozen different Indian gurus. There were ex-Catholics as well, and former Orthodox Jews. There was even a former Unitarian and, yes, even a former Jehovah's Witness. What we all had in common was a desire to read the Bible outside of a single religious context, and the willingness to share our varied perspectives and experiences along the way.

Seven years later we are still meeting every Thursday night. Babies have been born, members have come and gone, and sadly a few have died. And through it all we have gotten by with only two very simple rules:

1. We get to question anything.
2. We don't get to throw anything out.

Neither is particularly noteworthy in itself where Bible study is concerned. There are plenty of groups that observe one rule or the other. A purely secular reading of the Bible, for instance, allows us to question anything we read, while the fundamentalist reading preserves the literal meaning of the text. But the secular reading usually requires us to throw out whatever doesn't agree with its modernist approach to history or scientific fact, and the fundamentalist reading will not tolerate a diversity of opinions, or sometimes even questions.

Our group was, and continues to be, perhaps unique in allowing those two styles of reading to coexist. Indeed, we discovered in the interplay between those two readings of the Bible a kind of tension that led to spiritual breakthroughs. Then again, maybe we are not unique after all. There may be many such groups around the country at this point. It is an idea whose time has come; thus, nobody can lay claim to it as their own. After all, such a Bible study group is merely an externalization of the struggle that is already going on inside of anyone who wrestles for belief in God.

Which brings us back to Jacob and the angel.

The hidden lesson of the story is that it is all right to struggle for belief. Not only is it all right, sometimes it is even necessary that we begin from a place of confusion and doubt. Otherwise we will never know for certain whether our belief in God is real or counterfeit, full belief or only half.

In Jacob's case the wrestling goes on all night long. When the angel sees dawn approaching, he touches the inside of Jacob's thigh and his hip goes out of joint. And still Jacob won't let go. Finally, when the struggle has reached its peak, the angel asks Jacob's name and, when he hears it, says, "Thy name shall be called no more Jacob, but Israel: for as a prince hast thou power with God and with men, and hast prevailed" (Genesis 32:28).

The name *Israel* is the key to everything. Literally, it means "wrestles with God," but the spiritual sense is probably closer to "*willing* to wrestle." It refers to the person who commits to enduring the struggle between faith and doubt to the very end, the one who is willing to hold on until true belief is born. But that will never happen as long as we avoid the encounter by escaping into doubt—or if we withdraw early from the struggle, and declare faith the winner before we have truly fought. We must hang on until the end.

When Jacob does this, the angel tells him that he has "struggled with God and with men and has prevailed." But how is that possible? In the struggle between faith and doubt there can be no winner. We cannot make belief on our own. Only falling and being caught by God can make a believer. And that is the one thing we can never do for ourselves, no matter how long we fight or how tenaciously we hold on.

Finally, the battle itself is an illusion. Jacob experiences life as a struggle, as we all do, but the simple truth is, there is no safer place for Jacob than locked in the embrace of an angel. At the moment of wrestling he is *already* held by God. Belief comes at the moment he realizes this. And at that moment the battle is done. The sun rises to find him limping across the River Jabok to meet his destiny with an open heart, having named the place where he struggled with the angel Peniel, or "face of God." How appropriate.

8

The Name of God

And Moses said unto God, Behold, when I come unto the children
of Israel, and shall say unto them, The God of your fathers hath
sent me unto you; and they shall say to me, What is his name?
what shall I say unto them? And God said unto Moses, I Am That
I Am: and he said, Thus shalt thou say unto the children of Israel,
I Am hath sent me unto you.

—EXODUS 3:13–14

It should come as no surprise that Moses wants to put God inside a box—it's what we all do. Faced with the inexplicable, we immediately try to interpret it in terms of what we already know. What we know is words, and to reduce something to a word is always our first step in gaining control over it. Even the words "ineffable mystery" are just that, an attempt to affix a label to something we don't understand at all. That is why God answers Moses as he does: "I Am That I Am." To call himself anything else would be to reduce the truth so far that the name would no longer have any relationship to the thing it described. To call himself anything else would be, in a sense, to utter a lie.

In Moses' case, that inexplicable mystery is a bush that burns but is never consumed. Tending his flock, Moses has turned aside from the path to witness this marvel, whereupon the voice of God calls to him from out of the bush, telling him that he has been chosen to deliver the Israelites from their bondage in Egypt. Moses hasn't expected anything like this and has no idea how to accomplish it, so he immediately starts trying to find a way out of his own particular wrestling match with God.

"Who am I, that I should go unto Pharaoh, and that I should bring forth the children of Israel out of Egypt?" he asks (Exodus 3:11). But, when it comes to the Bible, the answer to such questions is always the same. God himself will see that it is accomplished. Moses only has to go.

Finally, when it no longer seems possible to avoid his charge, Moses asks a seemingly simple question ("And when the Israelites ask, whom shall I say has sent me?"), only to receive an answer that is as mysterious and inexplicable as the vision of the bush.

"I Am That I Am." It's almost the same as not answering the question, the same as saying, "Just look at the bush and wonder! For if you cannot understand this—how the bush burns but is not burned up—how will you understand the full truth, for this is but the smallest particle of who I Am." The name is meant to open Moses' mind so wide it turns it inside out, not shut it down by giving him the illusion that there is some aspect of God he can control or understand.

Here are a few contemporary translations of the Name of God, selected more or less at random:

"I Shall Prove To Be What I Shall Prove To Be."
(NEW WORLD TRANSLATION)

"I Am The One Who Always Is."
(NEW LIVING TRANSLATION)

"I Am Who I Am."
(NEW INTERNATIONAL VERSION, NEW KING JAMES VERSION,
NEW REVISED STANDARD VERSION)

"I am he who is."

(NEW JERUSALEM BIBLE)

All of the above versions (except for the New World Translation of the Jehovah's Witnesses) include a footnote offering an alternate reading, the most common being "I Will Be What I Will Be." And so perhaps it is fair to say that most translators aren't exactly sure what it means. The Jewish Publication Society makes this particularly clear in its version when it refuses to translate the name at all, leaving readers to puzzle over the original Hebrew, *ehyeh asher ehyeh,* which—again, according to a footnote—might mean "I Am That I Am," "I Am Who I Am," "I Will Be What I Will Be," and so forth. In other words, no one knows for sure.

This doesn't mean that no one has ever hazarded a guess. Literally thousands of theologians and scholars have had a try at it over the millennia. Some say the "I Am" of Exodus, which later came to be written as *Yahweh,* means that God is Pure Being, or—to put a more modern, ecumenical slant on it—the "ground of being." Others, perhaps in an effort to reduce God to a more manageable, tribal set of proportions, claim it means that the God of Israel will be whatever he needs to be for the Jewish people, and still others that the name means God is eternal: "The One Who Always Is." There are even esoteric schools in Judaism that see in the Hebrew letters of the name the secret of the cosmos itself, which can be understood by meditating on them in a highly prescribed way. But none of these explanations really tells us anything more than what God told Moses. No one really knows.

Moses asked a question and the answer turned him inside out. No wonder he later gets so testy with the Israelites, who, like the rest of us, prefer to have everything visible and spelled out. He is called by a God whose very name is inconceivable to do a job (delivering the Israelites from bondage) that is impossible but yet somehow gets done because of

God, then is led into a desert and finally up a mountain to talk with a God whose face, close as it must be in these encounters, he is never allowed to see. The amazing thing is that he believes in such a God and does everything that God wants him to do. It must be that being "turned inside out," while making it impossible to hold on to anything, nevertheless opens the mind to God. And so, even though Moses cannot conceive of such a God, much less actually see him, he nevertheless somehow feels himself within God's grasp and therefore knows that he is there.

But this is not where the story ends. If it were only true that God is unknowable, even through his name, then we would have little hope of ever believing in him, even if, like Moses, we could find ourselves somehow mystically turned inside out. The other half of the story is that, once given a name for God, we may call upon him from that moment forward, whether we know what his name means or not.

A person's name comes to mean something over the course of our relationship with that person. In the beginning, even the name of someone as significant as a spouse or child doesn't have much meaning in itself. Names are useful right from the outset, however, as a way of thinking about people, or keeping track of them, or talking about them with others. With time, however, even the mention of a person's name calls to mind certain thoughts and feelings.

In the case of God, the more we come to believe in him, the more powerful the effect of his name is upon us—even if that name is not in the original Hebrew, or even a version of that name, but only the simple word "God" or "Lord." We may have no idea what the ultimate meaning of such a word is; nevertheless, it means a great deal to us. In fact, in the end it may come to mean more than any other word we know. It becomes the name we call when we are lost, or hopeful, or thankful, or simply when we don't know where else to turn. It may be the first name we cry when danger is upon us, and the name we call with our final breath.

I once had a deeply moving experience of the power of the Name with a woman who until the very end of her life had never professed any belief in God. For that matter, when she finally did profess belief, it was only in the most oblique possible way. "Pray for me," she told my wife. It was the last thing she ever said to her.

My mother-in-law had come to stay with us the year before, when it became clear that she could no longer live alone in the town just south of Cape Cod where she'd spent most of her adult life. She'd been diagnosed with congestive heart disease the year before and, due to vascular dementia, had experienced increasingly long spells of disorientation that made us fearful for her safety. She could no longer remember whether she'd taken her pills or eaten breakfast, and then one morning her doctor called to tell us that she'd shown up four hours early for an appointment. For some reason the nurse was in the office very early that day, perhaps to catch up on paperwork, and heard her knocking. It was 6 a.m.

Pat had been a difficult woman in many ways. She could be stubborn and imperious. But that last year with us something happened and she finally seemed to let go and really trust other people for the first time in her life. We'd been worried that the strain of having her live with us would be too great, and truth is, it was sometimes very hard. But it wasn't because she was difficult. She was slowly dying and there was nothing anyone could do about it, and that was hard for everyone.

Her liver gave out in the end (the price of taking so many heart medications, no doubt), and she slipped into a coma. But the nurse on duty, a large Caribbean woman who'd midwifed countless people into the hereafter, assured us that Pat could still hear everything we said, and so we spent the evening talking to her and saying our good-byes.

But good-byes are two-sided. Difficult as it was for us to say good-bye to her, it seemed just as difficult for her to say good-bye to us. And so at a certain point, when the rest of the family had left and even my wife had interrupted her vigil for a short while, I spoke to her for a long time about that Power Beyond the Self that catches us when we fall.

Still she fought it, struggling for breath, often sighing or moaning with the strain of it all. And then it occurred to me that though she might have come to some sort of belief in the end, a confidence that all would be well, and all manner of thing would be well, she still might not have a name for it. I'd spoken in terms of God and Other Power, but maybe these meant nothing to her. And so, although now I can't say what possessed me to do such a thing, I began to recite one after another every name for God I had ever heard in my life and every prayer associated with them until I could think of nothing more—everything from the Lord's Prayer to the Heart Sutra.

Finally, having come full circle, I returned to one of the oldest names of all—YHWH, the one used by Moses. There is no way now to know why that name had the effect it did, but as I began to recite the letters very slowly next to her ear . . . *yod* . . . *hey* . . . *vav* . . . *hey* . . . she grew calmer and calmer, until finally she let out a great sigh and at that moment my wife came back to the room. She asked me to drive her sister home so she could get some rest. But the moment we got out of the car, we learned that Pat had gone. She'd died in her daughter's arms not moments after I'd left the room.

Moses is the first person in the Bible to ask the name of God and, not coincidentally, the only person in the Bible ever referred to as "God's friend." He is therefore the model for anyone whose aim is closeness with God. And where does that closeness begin? With the name.

There are some whose belief in a particular name for God is stronger than their belief in God himself. They have forgotten the first truth about God's name: that it is essentially unknowable. Believing that they know the correct name of God—whether it be YHWH, Vishnu, Allah, Lord, or Jesus Christ—they "take possession" of that name, wrapping it tightly in layer upon layer of self-importance, rather than letting it turn them inside out. The result is that the One God spoken of in the Bible is lost, to be replaced with something far smaller and more manageable that can be bent to our own personal will, or to the broader will of the tribe.

Others have forgotten the second truth. They may very well have been turned inside out by the thought of God—a thought too big to contemplate—but they find themselves unable to relate to God in a simple, personal way. Such people feel very comfortable with the various modern meanings attributed to the name of God—for instance, they may feel quite comfortable thinking of God in terms of Being, or Pure Spirit, or even Nothingness. But they won't feel comfortable saying "Jesus," "Abba," or "Lord."

To find friendship with God, like Moses we must remain open to both truths at once. We must be sophisticated enough to know that God is unknowable, and simple enough to come before him like a child. To choose one over the other is to miss the opportunity given us for deepening our belief. For those we believe in most deeply are those most deeply known.

9

The Golden Calf

And when the people saw that Moses delayed to come down
out of the mount, the people gathered themselves together
unto Aaron, and said unto him, Up, make us gods, which shall
go before us; for as for this Moses, the man that brought us up
out of the land of Egypt, we wot not what is become of him.

—EXODUS 32:1

Why is it so easy to have faith in one moment, and then so impossibly difficult in the next? Consider the act of waiting, as the Israelites do, for someone to arrive.

A few years ago my wife was asked to give a nominating speech at the local Democratic caucus, a big event in Woodstock, where politics is the major sport. She'd told me she would be back at ten—eleven at the latest—but by midnight she still wasn't home. The event was being held at a theater a mere four miles away, the weather was fine, and the roads between there and our house were straight and fairly easy to navigate. But by one o'clock I was a mess. By one-thirty I thought, What if she's dead, the victim of some freak highway accident? Could I raise the kids alone? We'd bought a term-life policy the year before, so the money wouldn't be a problem, not at first anyway. But I was worse than incompetent at most of the practicalities of family life. I could run a Zen monastery easily enough, but I always burned the grilled cheese and my kids simply refused to drink the cocoa I made on those rare occasions when it was a snow day and Perdita was nowhere to be found. I called the police only to be told that no accidents had been reported. Okay, so I could check that off the list. Next I began to imagine a fire at the theater, so I called back and asked if there'd been a problem at the caucus.

"The Democratic caucus?" asked the dispatcher. "Now *that's* something worth worrying about. I heard there was some name-callin' that ended in a fistfight. That may have slowed things up a bit. She'll probably be along home just as soon as they get done deciding who they're gonna run for treasurer."

Great, I thought. So it was a riot. At least there hadn't been a fire or a car accident. And a few minutes later Perdita walked in, took one look at my face, and said, "My God! Were you really that worried? Well, have no fear. No more caucuses for me. That was nuts!"

If we have been told that a family member will be home by ten o'clock at night, then up until that time we go along with our business, secure in the belief that all is well. Once ten o'clock has come and gone, however, we may begin to worry. If they still haven't arrived by eleven, most of us will begin to fear, and by midnight will be convinced that something has gone very wrong. What we believed in one moment, we find impossible to believe the next.

This is a fairly realistic portrait of the faith most of us have when we begin the struggle for belief. As long as things are going reasonably well, it is easy to believe. But that sort of belief is virtually guaranteed to fail, because things don't always go reasonably well. In fact, sometimes they don't go well at all. In such moments, we may remember Julian's motto that all shall be well and find some comfort there. But the mere fact that we have to remind ourselves of this indicates that we aren't Julian.

This must be the "sin" of the Israelites. It isn't so much what they do or make that causes the trouble, but the fact that they feel the need to make or do anything in the first place. Moses is up the mountain, about to come down. Or maybe not. Maybe he is dead. They don't know which, and they are never asked to know. They are only asked to believe in the ultimate outcome—that everything will work out optimally, in accordance with God's divine plan.

Of course, the Israelites don't do that; they draw up their own set of plans instead. God wants to create Israel in the deserts of the Sinai, but Israel keeps trying to create itself. Like the Israelites, again and again we are faced with the same lesson: allow yourself to be created in God's image and there is never any fear of creating an idol; try to create yourself, and there's nothing you can make that *isn't* one.

On its surface the story of the Golden Calf seems to be about how we shouldn't make idols, and about what happens when we do. But it doesn't explain what an idol really is, apart from the golden statue the Israelites create as a substitute for God.

Idols are a response to anxiety, and anxiety is born when we believe only in our own power and therefore put ourselves in God's place. This is so much the rule of life that we scarcely even notice doing it anymore. In that sense a story like that of the Golden Calf is misleading, because it seems to suggest that creating an idol is an extraordinary affair, and therefore something we would almost certainly notice ourselves doing, when in fact we do it automatically, without giving it a single thought.

A teenager is late in coming home. She's responsible enough in her own right, but her friends are another matter, and one of them is at the wheel tonight. Once our anxiety about this fact has set in, an idol is almost certain to make its appearance, and that is the idol we call God. By all rights that God should be referred to with a small *g*, because the god we appeal to at such moments is the creation of our own anxiety and not

God himself. You might call him the traffic god, the "Saint Christopher" god, or the god of safe travel, and because his scope and vision have been thus limited, it begins to seem possible to make a special plea with him for the safety of our child.

To such a god it seems possible to pray, "Of the teenagers on the road tonight, some of whom must suffer accidents, let my own child not be among them." Such a prayer becomes absurd if offered to the one Jews call *Ribonno Shel Olam,* the "Master of the Universe" who orders all things for the best. About that One God, Jesus tells us: "Your Father knoweth what things ye have need of, before ye ask him" (Matthew 6:8). *And all shall be well, and all manner of thing shall be well.* What is needed, first and last of all, is trust. Unfortunately, when we are that anxious, this is nearly impossible. In most cases, we can't even fake it.

The thing that most defines humankind is free will, our ability to determine things for ourselves, sometimes also called "the will to power." In essence, that means we always believe there is something we can do. Even when there isn't, and we get that sinking feeling that things have got completely beyond our control, we create an idol as a way of reclaiming some sense of power—or at least the illusion of it—because an idol is subject to our manipulation, while God himself is not.

That doesn't mean God doesn't answer our prayers. In fact, it means just the opposite—that God is *always* answering our prayers. There is never a moment when our prayers are *not* being answered by God, but because we do not ultimately know what is good or bad for us, we are hopelessly confused about what we truly need and want. Our perspective is limited. And so we struggle. Occasionally we are in sync enough with life to know in our hearts what we need and to pray for that, and at such moments the answer to our prayers is already on its way.

The God of all things, who keeps count of the hairs on our heads and knows the proper orbit of the planets and what black holes are for—that

God is forever beyond the power of our influence. Then again, God being what he is, there is no need for our influence. We are sustained by powers beyond our control or comprehension in virtually every second of our lives. And when indeed the end does come, and the body is cast off like a stone, God is the only one who can possibly keep track of our place in the ultimate scheme of things and is therefore the only one who can save us. However much we might wish it were otherwise, we exist only by the power of divine will. Even Jesus experiences this. On the night before the crucifixion he prays in the Garden of Gethsemane, "Father, if thou be willing, remove this cup from me: nevertheless not my will, but thine, be done" (Luke 22:42), surrendering to the grace of a power beyond his own.

Idols are supported by the belief that some prayers are answered while others are not. This is exactly the same as saying that some people are saved while others are damned. In each case the spiritual logic is the same. There is the belief that God saves those who behave in a certain manner, in accordance with certain religious rules or norms rather than behaving in accordance with others. But such a belief is based, not on one's faith in a loving, all-powerful God, but on the anxious manipulations of a limited god who can be convinced to champion the cause of one part of his creation over and above another. And that "small *g*" god is always an idol, even when he is referred to as Yahweh, Allah, or Our Lord Jesus Christ.

In the end, our tribal rituals and customs become idols because we put them between ourselves and God—because, however connected to God they might have been in the beginning, they always end up becoming a thing of their own. And this is the case not only for those rituals and customs that have a specifically religious origin. It also applies to governments, empires, kingdoms, and the like.

When Moses does finally come back down the mountain, he finds a peculiar scene unfolding at the foot of Mount Sinai. Under the leadership of his brother, Aaron, the Israelites have fashioned an idol from the collective gold of their various earrings. When Moses sees this, he says to Aaron, "What did this people unto thee, that thou hast brought so great a sin upon them?" (Exodus 32:21).

Aaron explains that the people have become fearful because Moses—their figurehead, their god-in-place-of-God—has been so long in coming down from the mountain. Finally, in their anxiety, they have demanded that something be done. "And I said unto them, Whosoever hath any gold, let them break it off. So they gave it me: then I cast it into the fire, and there came out this calf" (Exodus 32:24).

This is at once a lie (presumably the gold did not mold itself spontaneously into the shape of a calf) and a profound truth about how idols are made, because—indeed—we don't have to think about them to create them. In fact, the less we think about what we are doing, the more effective the idol we create.

There are many examples in life of effective idols, idols that fulfill our needs so perfectly that we are apt to lose track of the fact that we have made them ourselves, but by far the most dangerous is the one we call "God," without realizing that the one whose power and authority we evoke is really just the self in disguise. This happens whenever we champion our God as the True God, in the process denying or excluding God as worshipped by our neighbor.

This happens for two simple reasons. The first is that competing claims to truth make us anxious; they make us doubt that the idol we have created for ourselves is truly the one all-powerful God. Second is that we really cannot conceive of the idea of One God, who is always present to all peoples in all cultures, a God beyond borders, beyond history even, who keeps watch over the birth, the life, and the death of all beings everywhere without exception. We cannot conceive of such a God, and so we reduce him to the more manageable size of an idol, which becomes a substitute for God. That idol can be convinced to protect democracy from communism, to champion the rights of Christians over Jews, or Jews over Muslims, or Muslims over Jews. It can be used to convince ourselves that only the Buddha's teachings are real and true, or that those who eat pork are damned. But always it remains simply what it is: not the One God of the Bible, inclusive of all people and all things, but an idol we have made to suit our purposes—for which we will suffer, and make others suffer as well.

10

The Death of Moses

And the Lord said unto him, This is the land which I sware
unto Abraham, unto Isaac, and unto Jacob, saying, I will give it
unto thy seed: I have caused thee to see it with thine eyes,
but thou shalt not go over thither.

—DEUTERONOMY 34:4

Think of a drop of water on its long, winding passage to the sea. It begins as a single snowflake somewhere in the mountains, where it remains for long, cold months awaiting spring. At last comes a day when the sun touches the snow above and all around it, steadily unbinding a clutch of bright trickles from the mountain stones. From there it is carefully ushered along with its fellows by the smallest grooves and patterns in the rock face until it meets that larger, more discernible pattern we call a stream, and onward until it finds the groove of a river, and still onward to the sea. That is, unless it evaporates. Unless it is lapped up by a snake, a beetle, a rabbit, or a deer. Unless it happens to seep through cracks in the bedrock and enter the groundwater of a spring. There are so many things that can happen to a drop of water. Only one thing is certain. Though it take a thousand years, it will always reach the ocean in the end.

At the end of his life, Moses is not allowed to enter the Promised

Land. On the day of his death, he is taken to the top of Mount Pisgah, where the Lord shows him the land pledged to Abraham and Isaac and Jacob. "I have caused thee to see it," says God, "but thou shalt not go over."

Ostensibly this is a punishment against Moses for having claimed God's power as his own. Earlier, when the Israelites were thirsty, God caused Moses to strike a rock with his staff, whereupon a stream of fresh water gushed forth. Later, when the people were thirsty again, Moses struck another rock, this time saying to the Israelites, "Hear now, ye rebels; must we fetch you water out of this rock?" (Numbers 20:10). Just as before, water rushed out, and the people and their animals were saved. But afterward God tells Moses that, because of this sin, he will never reach Canaan alive.

The logic is simple: Moses sinned, therefore Moses must be punished; and because Moses is no ordinary man but the leader of the Israelites, he must be punished in a spectacular and memorable way by being denied the very thing he has worked so hard to achieve. But while that logic is indeed very simple and straightforward, it is flawed from a spiritual point of view, for it overlooks the most fundamental truth in all of the Bible: that God orders all things for the best and can therefore be trusted in every conceivable situation, just as surely as the water can trust the path of the river on its way to the sea—even if it must cross a mountain or a desert, even if it must run the rapid and the waterfall and be shattered into a billion silver pieces on a stone.

All things happen by the will of God, and the will of God is optimal. There is no second-guessing it, and there is no way to subvert or misdirect it. The twentieth-century Buddhist poet Asahara Saichi understood it this way:

In the realm of Other Power
There is no Self Power

There is no Other Power
All *is Other Power.*

Like all of us, even Moses has a hard time accepting this truth. Faced with the loss of his greatest dream, he implores God repeatedly to be allowed to visit the Promised Land, if only for a single day. Finally, he is told to stop asking. In the end, he dies "at the word of the Lord," and is buried by God himself so that the place of his resting remains unknown, even to the present day. And that is where the Torah, the first five books of the Bible, ends.

But it is also where it begins again. In the yearly cycle of Torah readings observed by Jews, the readings are divided into weekly *parshiyot* (or portions), the last of which deals with the death of Moses, and the first, the creation of Adam. Thus the death of Moses is followed by the birth of Adam, and the whole cycle begins again.

If the Torah can be seen as a going forth in search of God, the last chapter is where we find him. But there is no obvious passage telling us so. Moses is denied entry to the Promised Land and promptly dies, and that is it. Except for a curious coincidence—the fact that the Torah begins and ends with a kiss.

The first kiss is easy to recognize. "And the Lord God formed man of the dust of the ground, and breathed into his nostrils the breath of life" (Genesis 2:7). It is the kiss of life that transforms mere dust into "a living soul." It is the imageless image of God, beyond presence or absence— eternal, uncreated, and yet the basis of all created things.

The second kiss is not so obvious—at least not in the English translation. "So Moses the servant of the Lord died there in the land of Moab, according to the word of the Lord" (Deuteronomy 34:5). In the original Hebrew, however, it says literally that Moses died "at the *mouth* of the Lord," giving rise to the ancient belief that God takes the breath of life back into himself at death with a kiss. We call this the end, but only because we cannot conceive of what it means to utterly entrust ourselves to God, to give back to God the breath we were given in the beginning as easily as we give back in every moment the breath we took from God just the moment before. All of life is dying—and all dying is being born again.

That is why the death of Moses is not the tragedy it could be, and the reason why death, which many of us secretly regard as a kind of final insult, is not the curse it seems to be, but the common blessing of all that lives.

We all die gazing at the Promised Land; Moses is not the exception, but the rule. Others will wake to cross over Jordan to the promise of another day—a son or daughter, a brother or beloved friend, while we must remain behind. We never know the end of the story. There is no need for us to know. The twentieth-century Zen master Zenkei Shibayama once wrote a beautiful poem about just this realization:

A flower blooms in silence, falls in silence,
And never returns to its stem.
In a moment, at just one place,
It forgoes all its life.
The voice of a flower,
The reality of the flower stem.
There the happiness of eternal life
Is shining without regret.

Again and again the Bible teaches us the wisdom of limits—that we are made mortal for a reason. How else could we appreciate the inestimable value of even a day? Without death, how could we know the price of a single breath of life? Without death how would surrender, and therefore union with God, be possible? Surely this is not something we could accomplish on our own, even in a thousand years, or in ten thousand.

It is our mistake to look for immortality in the span of years. It is only in the moment of finding our limit that we find God. Then, at last, we touch the infinite, and know that we are "wondrously made." This gift lies beyond even the grasp of the angels—yet the smallest flower is given it in full. The Promised Land is nothing in comparison. Having understood that, what need is there to go?

Practice

11

Hannah's Prayer

Now Hannah, she spake in her heart; only her lips moved,
but her voice was not heard: therefore Eli thought she had been
drunken. And Eli said unto her, How long wilt thou be drunken?
put away thy wine from thee. And Hannah answered and said,
No, my lord, I am a woman of a sorrowful spirit: I have drunk
neither wine nor strong drink, but have poured out my soul
before the Lord.

—1 SAMUEL 1:13–15

I once heard the story of a woman who'd gone on retreat at a Catholic convent. Not long after she arrived, she met with the abbess, who asked if she'd ever prayed before.

"No," the woman answered. "I've only done Zen meditation."

"Oh?" replied the abbess. "And who told you that wasn't prayer?"

When I heard this story, I thought I knew the answer to the abbess's question. More likely than not it had been some well-meaning religious type—some Christian priest or Buddhist monk. People tend to be possessive about the spiritual practices associated with their religion, the rules for observing them, and the precise manner in which they are to be done. If they can't control God exactly, at least they can control the means of access to him. But no, it seemed the woman in question had told *herself* they couldn't be the same. We all take these things too seriously, as if it were important which particular brand of ladder you used to escape from a house on fire, or with which foot, left or right, you stepped down upon the top rung. The important thing is getting out of the house before it burns.

In many ways, our life in this world is a burning house. Or, rather, that is how it seems to a self that is doomed to suffer annihilation and decay. Take a step beyond that house into the realm of that Power Beyond the Self we call God—even *one* step—and immediately we experience a very different kind of world. Buddhists call that world the Pure Land, Christians the kingdom of God. But it doesn't really matter which direction we go in—east or west—as long as we get out. The situation is urgent. Our lives are passing with every heartbeat and every breath, and nothing in life is certain but that it will pass. It usually takes a crisis of some sort to make this clear to us, however. The rest of the time we are content, as it were, to ignore the heat and smoke.

But, then, how do we take that single step beyond the burning house of the self?

On the day she goes to the temple to put her petition before God, Hannah is so distraught over her failure to conceive a child she seems drunk with it. Gone is her self-consciousness before others, gone even her awareness of what they will think. Even in the presence of Eli, the chief priest, she is utterly alone with God.

This is what it means to "speak in the heart." If it looks like drunkenness, that is because it is intoxicating to throw off pride and inhibition. If it seems slightly scandalous, that only shows how rare it is, even for a priest like Eli, to see someone pouring out her soul before God.

Hannah's is a very ancient prayer. It is the prayer of a mother for the gift of a child, the prayer of the farmer that a portion of his crops may be spared, the herdsman that the jackals be kept from his flock. And yet, opportunities for that kind of prayer are never lacking even today. They come to us in moments of extremity, when the good health we took for granted is suddenly lost, when we lose a job, a mother, or a spouse. Or when we truly need something—forgiveness, a fresh start, a reprieve from financial ruin—a need so bad it hurts. Only then are we able to call out to God from the depths of our being. It is only then, when we have emptied our souls of all that is extraneous or insincere, that at last we call from the bottom, and are answered from on high.

That is what Hannah means when she says that she has "poured out her soul before the Lord." She has poured out all her thoughts and feelings, wants and fears, letting them go, one after another, until there is nothing left to pour. This may seem a very Christian or Jewish practice on the face of it, but in reality it is far older than that. No one knows who invented it, and the many forms of religious devotion—contemplation, meditation, and other spiritual practices—have all evolved from this.

When I first tried to pray again after a lapse of more than thirty years, I was embarrassed by the very fact of talking to God. I sometimes feel that Western practitioners of Eastern traditions like yoga or meditation prefer those disciplines in part because, being silent, they are relatively tasteful and self-contained from a modern point of view. At least in my case I know that to be so. Spiritual practice is always a risk, and there is every chance that, if successful, it will trigger powerful emotions along the way, that it will eventually bring us to the point where there can be no more polite reserve, no tasteful holding back, because everything is finally on the line.

I reached that point in my own practice nine years ago, when a book I had been working on didn't sell. Actually, there was more to it than that. It was a book I shouldn't have been writing in the first place, on a subject I didn't understand and had no feel for, but which both my agent and editor at the time told me was solid gold. It was sure to fetch a six-figure advance, they assured me, and so ignoring common sense and a promise I'd made to myself some years earlier that I'd never write anything for money that wasn't real and true, I steeled myself to the task, maxing out all my credit cards for nine months running so that I could devote myself to working on it full-time.

My editor was embarrassed when her editorial board rejected the book, and my agent apologized profusely with each subsequent rejection, saying the whole thing was his fault. But it wasn't. I'd known all along I had no business writing a book that wasn't true.

By then it hardly mattered who was to blame. We were three months behind on the mortgage, with no money left from my previous book advances, and deeply in debt besides. The night after the final rejection came in and it was time to throw in the towel, I couldn't sleep with my wife and two young children. I was too ashamed. I went into the guest room and lay on top of the covers the whole night through, unable to move any part of my body or mind. When I think back on it, the only image I can come up with to describe my mental state at that time is being sealed inside a box the exact same dimensions as my body, except for a half inch on either side—enough wiggle room to understand that I was trapped alive but not enough to do anything about it.

When the sun rose, the spell was broken, and at last I was able to move. I got up off the bed and did something that would have seemed extremely peculiar to me only a day before. I went to the bookshelf in the hall and took down the Bible I had bought on impulse a few weeks earlier but hadn't yet cracked and, holding it against my forehead like a poultice, whispered, "All right, you win. I don't know where to go or what to do. I don't even know how to pray." And I opened the Bible to a page at random and read the first words I saw: "Then said I, Ah, Lord God! behold, I cannot speak: for I am a child. But the Lord said unto me, Say not, I am a child: for thou shalt go to all that I shall send thee, and whatsoever I command thee thou shalt speak" (Jeremiah 1:6–7).

After that I could pray. Having confessed my limits, and my difficulty with prayer itself, it was as if the lid I'd been wrestling with for years was finally off the jar. "Arise!" says Jeremiah. "Cry out in the night: in the beginning of the watches pour out thine heart like water before the face of the Lord" (Lamentations 2:19). That was what I did. And Jeremiah was right: it all poured out of me, just like water from a glass.

Westerners who practice Eastern spiritual disciplines like Zen meditation often find them easy to learn but difficult to master. They are taught to sit quietly in a relaxed upright position, focusing their awareness on each breath as it comes and goes from the body, letting thoughts pass freely to and from the stage of the mind. In most cases, however, they aren't taught how to entrust themselves to that process—how, as the thirteenth-century Japanese Zen Master Dogen put it, to "throw body and mind into the house of Buddha, so that all is done by Buddha." That kind of wholehearted surrender cannot be effected by an effort of concentration. It takes belief in Buddha, just as prayer takes belief in God.

That being said, prayer is also the *practice* of believing in God and not just the fruit of that practice. To begin with, we don't have to have any belief at all. There is a beautiful line to that effect from the Persian poet Rumi: "If you cannot pray sincerely, offer your dry, hypocritical, /agnostic prayer, for God in His mercy accepts bad coin." The important thing is to raise the closed lid of the heart. As the water flows—and it is *only* water, however we may feel about it, good coin or bad—the lid will eventually loosen and the flow become as natural as breathing.

When I first began this practice, I followed the advice of Reb Nachman of Breslov, the eighteenth-century Hasidic rabbi who taught his disciples to speak to God in their own language without any intermediary, "as if to a true good friend." This was the form of "meditation" he advocated, more ancient than the Bible itself. Reb Nachman spoke of enlisting the aid of the grasses of the field in this pursuit and would wander the countryside in prayer, inspired by the wonder of creation. Once when he was out walking with his disciple Reb Noson, he swept his hand in a gesture that took in all the hills and fields about them and remarked, "There is no place out there I haven't prayed." Of course, this could be taken as a kind of spiritual boast, a claim to the life of continuous prayer. But I think it was really a teaching in disguise. Reb Nachman meant there should be no aspect of our lives uninformed by our conversation with God—there should be no place in our lives we haven't prayed.

In its most basic form, prayer is as simple as thinking, only instead of keeping our thoughts private, we open them to God. The Buddhist saint Honen once explained it this way. The moon shines everywhere across the land, and there is no place its light is not reflected: in lakes and rivers, streams and puddles, even in the smallest teacup. But only if the lid is removed.

This is the point of the earliest story of the Bible. When Adam and Eve ate from the tree of the knowledge of good and evil, their first act was to cover their nakedness and hide themselves from God:

> *And they heard the voice of the Lord God walking in the garden in the cool of the day: and Adam and his wife hid themselves from the presence of the Lord God amongst the trees of the garden.*
>
> *And the Lord God called unto Adam, and said unto him, Where art thou?*
>
> *And he said, I heard thy voice in the garden, and I was afraid, because I was naked; and I hid myself.*
>
> *And he said, Who told thee that thou wast naked?*
>
> (GENESIS 3:8–11)

"Who told you that you were naked?" God asks. But he knows the answer already. They have told themselves. It is the beginning of private thought, the beginning of good and evil, the beginning of the self.

In their natural state, all beings are naked before God. "Consider the lilies of the field, how they grow," says Jesus, "they toil not, neither do they spin: And yet I say unto you, That even Solomon in all his glory was not arrayed like one of these" (Matthew 6:28–29). What can we add to the image of God? Any clothing, any covering whatsoever, will only hide it. We create the self to protect the self, adding layer upon layer of self-importance in the deluded belief that by doing so we can somehow effect our own deliverance. But it doesn't work. We are saved already. Only we don't know this, because we don't know who we really are. This is the purpose of practice—to recover the knowledge of a flower, the knowledge of the grasses of the field. But to do that we must first stop hiding from God.

There are as many ways of doing that as there are things to hide behind, and thus each religious culture offers practices of its own to help us get out from behind the fig leaf, but they all come down to this in the end: lifting the lid of the self and pouring ourselves out like water before the face of the Lord. "Who told you that Zen meditation wasn't prayer?" said the abbess. She might just as easily have said, "Who told you that you were naked? Who told you there was any moment when you weren't in conversation with God?"

12

Five Smooth Stones

And he took his staff in his hand, and chose him five smooth
stones out of the brook, and put them in a shepherd's bag which
he had, even in a scrip; and his sling was in his hand: and
he drew near to the Philistine.

—1 SAMUEL 17:40

What does it look like to believe in God? Ask twenty people that question, and you are likely to get twenty different answers—everything from going to church on Sunday to voting Republican (or Democrat) to working in a soup kitchen feeding the poor. Or, if you happen upon someone a little more ambitious, the answer might be following all the laws of the Torah, facing Mecca five times daily, or spending an hour or more each morning in contemplative prayer. But do these really tell us that a person believes in God?

Plenty of people feed the poor, observe religious laws and customs, and even spend time in prayer merely in order to feel good about themselves. Perhaps they were raised with the idea that this is what a good person does. Or perhaps they believe that it is within their power to influence their own salvation—that by behaving in a religiously prescribed way they can be assured of finding favor with God. But that is not the same as belief. What such people believe in is not God's power, but their power over God.

It is one of the most difficult, but essential discoveries of the spiritual life that most of our efforts to practice religion are nothing but Self Power in disguise. It is hard to realize, for instance, that our daily conversation with the Divine, in whatever form that takes, may be a way of trying to save ourselves that finally has little or nothing to do with God.

So what *does* belief in God look like? And what does it look like to *practice* that belief? Is it something we are even capable of recognizing in ourselves or in another? I think the answer is yes, but not because it looks in any way "special" or "different" from the rest of life. Belief is distinguished by its very simplicity, by the fact that it looks exactly like an ordinary life on any given day. It is recognizable by its failure to distinguish itself as special.

Consider one of the most memorable stories from the Bible: the battle between the shepherd boy David and the Philistine Goliath, whose spear was so heavy it could not even be lifted by any other man. On its surface the story is anything but ordinary, fighting a giant in single combat not being on the agenda for your average day. But David's response to that situation, rooted firmly in his belief in God, makes it so. When King Saul protests that a mere boy, unschooled in the art of battle, cannot possibly succeed against a seasoned warrior such as Goliath, David explains that in the past the Lord has helped him prevail against a lion and a bear who came to attack his flock.

Saul tries to convince David to accept his armor for protection, but after trying it on, David decides that it's better left behind. Then Saul offers him his sword. But David rejects this, too. He isn't used to it. And it's too heavy. In the end he goes into battle with nothing but his staff and shepherd's sling. But first he stops to choose five smooth stones from the brook.

Five smooth stones . . .

When David defeats Goliath a few verses later, he uses only the first of these stones. So why the other four? Is his faith in God less absolute than he would have us believe? And if not, why go into battle with more than the single stone he needs?

Among the works of different rabbis and theologians, we find a variety of answers. Some attribute a special symbolic significance to the number five. Others observe that it would have been prideful to carry only one. Still others say the number is entirely random. But what if five was simply the number of stones David usually carried in his bag? What if David goes forth to meet the giant in exactly the same way he goes forth each morning into the hills to pasture his sheep?

Belief in God requires no fanfare, nor any special protection. Belief itself—in God and in the life we have been given—is finally the only protection we need.

After her mother's death, my wife, Perdita, found a number of ways of managing her grief. One was taking long daily runs through the mountains, another was reading the Bible from cover to cover, and still another was getting regular treatments from a local woman who came highly recommended as a massage therapist. They forgot to mention that she was also a newly converted and deeply enthusiastic member of a local Pentecostal church that had been started a few years earlier by a former rock musician.

In the blasted-wide-open state of grieving for a parent, Perdita was probably ripe for some sort of conversion, or at least consolation, and so I don't think it's fair to say that her massage therapist's spiritual overtures came entirely unsolicited. Besides which, our family religious culture is such that we're always open to learning about other spiritual paths. At that time we were entertaining the Jehovah's Witnesses every Thursday morning to learn about their method of Bible study, and one day the week before I'd come home from writing at a café to discover a Chinese

Pure Land master I'd never met drinking tea on the floor with my children and teaching them the rudiments of *qi-gong*. But when Amy (not her real name) began advising Perdita to put on the full armor of God each morning as soon as she woke so that she could "take her stand against the devil," Perdita began to feel uneasy. Quoting Ephesians 6, Amy spoke further of "the belt of truth," "the breastplate of righteousness," "the shield of faith," "the helmet of salvation," and the "sword of spirit." In all, a lot of armor—and at least one outright weapon, which, like Saul's sword, might prove too heavy to lift.

"Isn't the armor of God just what Adam and Eve wore in the garden?" Perdita later asked me. "Ephesians notwithstanding, it seems to me like all that armor is the problem, not the solution."

Belief is the only ordinary commodity in a world entirely given over to its opposite, which is the battle between faith and doubt. That battle drives us to all kinds of extremes at every level of society. The Buddhist saint Shinran once said, "If the conditions are right, we human beings will do anything!" He meant that we will go to any lengths to protect ourselves—and not just our lives, but our beliefs, opinions, and even our ideas. We will imprison innocent people on the basis of their race or religion, champion the rights of unborn children while starving or bombing the children of our enemy, and build up military spending at the expense of programs that benefit the sick, the elderly, or the poor. That is why true belief is easy to recognize. It takes the middle way. It isn't deceived by the struggle between faith and doubt, even as it rages within and all around us, but instead seeks the only real alternative—entrusting ourselves to God, confused and inconstant as we are. That is the genesis of true belief and the reason it looks so plain. It doesn't protect itself, or project itself onto others, making them into angels or demons. It takes us as we are, stick and sling, and works its magic with that.

In the end, it isn't a matter of how much or how little faith David has that God will help him defeat the giant. He still doesn't know how many stones it will take. He still doesn't know how much, or for how long, God expects him to fight. Like David, we are creatures with free will, with the capacity for independent thought and action, and that must play into any and all endeavors we undertake in this world—including spiritual ones. Saichi says, "All is Other Power," but that doesn't change the fact that we experience things primarily in terms of a self.

So the question becomes this: Given that the self is what we have to work with, what kind of spiritual practice contributes to belief in God?

There is no easy answer to this question, but there is a *simple* one—simple in the sense of becoming innocent and even childlike before God. Simple because it requires no outward change, no donning of heavy armor, no cultivation of any new religious impulses or norms. We don't have to order meditation cushions, throw out the food in our refrigerator, or change the way we speak or dress. We just set off in the clothes we stand up in, with the resources we already have. Once the conversation with God is under way, we will be told everything we need to know, *as* we need to know it. And *if* we need to know.

That is what is so beautiful about the moment in the story when David stoops down at the brook to gather five stones for his scrip. God is with him; nevertheless he takes the usual number of stones. How long will he have to fight? He doesn't know. How much of the outcome will be determined by his skill with the sling and how much by God? There is no way to separate the two. There is no Self Power. There is no Other Power. *All* is Other Power. Even when the story is over and the giant lies dead at his feet, there is no clear line dividing David from the one he calls "the Living God."

13

David Dances Before the Ark

And David danced before the Lord with all his might; and
David was girded with a linen ephod. So David and all the house
of Israel brought up the ark of the Lord with shouting, and
with the sound of the trumpet.

—2 SAMUEL 6:14–15

When we look at our own lives and those of the people around us, we
don't have to look very far to find proof of the old adage "Sometimes bad
things happen to good people." A seven-year-old child without a care in
the world is suddenly afflicted with a headache and dies of an aneurysm
before she can reach the hospital. A man who has spent his whole life car-
ing for the poor is brutally beaten in a ghetto and left for dead. At such
times, we tend to fall back on the belief that such things happen for a reason that, if we had all the facts, could be explained—for, as we all know,
a misfortune that can be explained could often have been avoided. Didn't
the child in question report feeling dizzy just the month before? Hadn't
the man who was beaten wandered into a neighborhood where the people didn't know his work? But of course such explanations seem hollow,
based as they are on the implied criticism "Had we been wiser and

smarter . . ." The problem is, even when we are good and play by all the rules, we still aren't omniscient. We aren't wise. We aren't even smart. And that goes for everybody, even David.

The Ark of the Covenant, containing the tablets received by Moses on Mount Sinai, was the holiest of all holy objects to the Jews. For many centuries, we are told, it went wherever they did. Where they came to rest, it was enshrined in a portable temple called the Tabernacle; when they traveled, it was carried on long gold-covered poles made from acacia wood. They even carried it into battle as a protective talisman and a symbol of their righteousness, a kind of holy banner. And that was how, on one occasion, it came to be captured by the Philistines. The Philistines, however, were unhappy with the ark, which caused their idols to fall over and produced tumors on their bodies, so they returned it to Israel, where it was kept at the house of Abinadab in Kirjath-jearim.

Resolving to return the ark to its rightful place in Jerusalem, David, now the king of Israel, traveled to Kirjath-jearim and had his men place it on an oxcart. Soon, however, the oxen stumbled and, seeing that the ark was about to fall to the ground, a man named Uzzah put out his hand to steady it and died at once by the hand of the Lord. At first David was angry, then afraid. "How shall the ark of the Lord come to me?" he asked (2 Samuel 6:9), and when no answer was forthcoming, he left the ark at the home of a man named Obededom for three months and returned to Jerusalem for further reflection.

In a later version of the story, David discovers a reason for the shocking death of Uzzah. "None ought to carry the ark of God but the Levites: for them hath the Lord chosen to carry the ark of God, and to minister unto him for ever" (1 Chronicles 15:2), he explains to the Israelites. And, indeed, on consulting the book of the law, they discover that the Lord had instructed Moses in the proper handling of the ark. It was to be moved on the shoulders of the priestly tribe of Israel. Having discovered the correct ritual observance, complete with scriptural precedent, David returns to the home of Obededom, and all goes according to plan.

But that can't be the point of the story—the mere observance of proper ritual. If that is all spiritual practice is about, then it becomes nothing but an exercise in Self Power, for all such ritual observances, whatever their symbolic or practical value, are merely ways of trying to influence God, a kind of spiritual body English we can't help using, even when we secretly suspect it doesn't work. But if not ritual, then what *is* the point? Shocking as it may seem, the point of the story seems to be that, even with the very best intentions, it is sometimes inevitable to be zapped by God. The question then becomes, How do I live with that?

If one saw a precious sacred object about to fall upon the ground, possibly to be harmed or destroyed, who wouldn't unthinkingly put out a hand to keep it from falling? Wouldn't the person whose instinct it was to let it fall be more at fault? These must have been some of the thoughts in David's mind when Uzzah died. Can we blame him for feeling angry at the Lord? But then, how is he going to go on living in a world where all things are in the hands of God? Seen in that light, David's question "How shall the ark of the Lord come to me?" is not just a matter of finding the right procedure. It's far more dire than that. The real question is "How can the Lord come into the heart of one who is so angry and afraid?"

This is a question that each of us, at one point or another in life, will be forced to ask. Faced with the inevitable (old age), the inexplicable (sickness), or the unfathomable (death itself), will we not be forced to appeal to the very God who, in fashioning us from the dust of the ground, has "made us that way"? This is the question David faces when Uzzah puts forth his hand to stay the ark. It takes three months to answer it, and when he does, the answer changes him. He is a different person than he was before, and to express that change he does something unprecedented. Stripping down to his loincloth, he dances naked with joyous abandon before all Israel as the ark is brought into the city. It is the only way the ark can come back to Jerusalem, David realizes, and the only way *he* can come back to *God.*

But this all happened long ago, and in the Bible no less, which to some people means that it probably didn't happen at all, or if it did, that it doesn't happen anymore. But of course that isn't true. We only have to look around us to see Uzzahs dying and Davids dancing—everywhere we go.

What do we do when terrible events interrupt the conversation with God? Over the years I have been asked more times than I can remember how a loving God could allow the Holocaust, the killing fields, or even the death of a single child. How do we talk to such a God? And do we *want* to talk to him?

Not long after our son Jonah stopped sleeping in the crib next to our bed, we decided to have a yard sale. The crib, a hand-me-down from a friend of a friend, was a real monstrosity—sturdy and nice enough looking, but much too big and heavy for our bedroom. Besides which, the slats kept coming loose. In any case, we'd discovered we were much happier (and slept better) all in the same bed. And so we put a notice in the paper to this effect:

> *Young family unburdening itself of TONS of formerly useful things that we've now outgrown but your growing family might want or need—all at ROCK BOTTOM PRICES!!!*

And that was how we met Bar Scott.

A beautiful thirtyish woman in a loose-fitting sundress, and about eight months pregnant, she looked familiar in the way that professional singers or actresses often do, even when you've never actually seen them before. She arrived to look at the crib and after she had checked it out thoroughly, we arrived at a price and she arranged to pick it up later with her husband, Peter, who was handy with tools and could "fix those slats up in a jiff."

The transfer of goods was a comic dumb show in itself, with me on the upstairs balcony of our bedroom trying to lower the crib down on a rope like some overweight angel at a Christmas play, while various directors and stagehands whispered fierce, if conflicting, directives. But somehow, together, we all managed to get it down and the crib was theirs.

Not so long after that, I saw Bar and her son, Forrest, in town and couldn't help but think that she was one of the most earnest and devoted mothers I'd ever met. I remember one long conversation we had about the family bed, about how researchers had discovered that in cultures where babies slept with their parents, the incidence of sudden infant death syndrome was far lower (apparently that clunky crib with its loose slats had made believers out of her and Peter as well). Bar was starting a group to raise awareness about the issue and wanted to get a bunch of mothers together to share their experiences.

I never found out about the mothers' group, whether she started it or not. I suspect that, like a lot of new mothers, she discovered there weren't enough hours in the day. In any case, I'd see her and Forrest around town at one point or another almost every week and would wave and say hi. And somehow that seems to be the way it always goes: one day you're waving to each other at the drop-off for preschool, the next, one of your children has cancer and life is turned upside down.

Forrest's cancer was a life-changing experience, not only for Bar and Peter but for much of the town as well. It was hard to imagine how such a sweet, innocent young child could be afflicted with such an aggressive cancer. Hard to fathom the courage and resilience of his parents. Hard to understand it when, after several miraculous occurrences that seemed like reprieves or at least remissions, he suddenly worsened one day and quickly died the next. I think it is fair to say that the conversation with God was very earnest in Woodstock that year and even heated in the end.

The whole town turned out for the funeral service, converging for the long walk over the hill through the town cemetery on a cold, diamond-bright day. Peter, handy with tools, had stayed up all the night before making a simple but beautiful coffin for his son. And Bar, whose training as a performer had served her well in putting on a brave face during some of the darker moments of the previous months, was worn to a fierce, transparent clarity that concealed nothing, and poured out of her like water from the world's oldest, deepest well as she sang, "Amazing grace, how sweet the sound." Her voice was as beautiful as I've ever heard it. There was nothing sweet about it, nothing sweet at all. But like Shibayama's flower and David's dancing, it was utterly real and joyous and true.

14

A Handful of Meal

And she said, As the Lord thy God liveth, I have not a cake,
but a handful of meal in a barrel, and a little oil in a cruse:
and, behold, I am gathering two sticks, that I may go in and
dress it for me and my son, that we may eat it, and die.

—1 KINGS 17:12

Belief is counterintuitive. From an ordinary standpoint, it makes no sense. Who would ask a starving widow for food? For that matter, what mother would give bread to a perfect stranger when she couldn't even feed her son? But the prophet Elijah has been told by God that a certain widow in Zarephath will feed him, and indeed she does—even though she has almost nothing to give.

If the first part of the Bible is about giving the knowledge of good and evil back to God, the second part is about giving up calculation—the countless ways we have of hedging our bet with God or the universe so that we come out on top more often than not. It is about giving up the habit of tailoring our thoughts and deeds in such a way as to maximize, or simply protect, our sense of self.

Elijah the Tishbite has been called by God to deliver a message to

King Ahab that a great drought is on the way. Then he is sent into the wilderness to live by a certain brook where he is to be fed by ravens. Eventually the stream dries up, however, and God sends him to the poor widow instead.

The Bible is almost comical sometimes in the way it portrays God. Elijah must have assumed that if he was being sent to get food from a widow in Zarephath, she would *have* some food. To arrive only to discover that she is in the act of preparing her very last meal, scant as it is, must surely take him by surprise. If so, however, he recovers right away.

Don't be afraid, Elijah tells her. Just do as you have planned. Only first, make a little cake of meal and bring it to me; then make the rest for you and your son, and it will be all right. And indeed it is. "And the barrel of meal wasted not, neither did the cruse of oil fail, according to the word of the Lord, which he spake by Elijah" (1 Kings 17:16).

Belief is the central mystery of the spiritual life. With it, all things are possible. Without it, nothing is. This is the meaning of Jesus' words "For he that hath, to him shall be given: and he that hath not, from him shall be taken even that which he hath" (Mark 4:25). Is this not the real meaning of the handful of meal and the little bit of oil that the widow has left in her store? Isn't that really what Elijah recognizes when he sees her? An ordinary person would see poverty; a selfish person, that she had nothing much to give. But Elijah, "the man of God," sees the spark of belief. He fans that spark, and suddenly it's enough for everybody. It is *always* more than enough.

In the Bible, we often find stories and parables that have as their central lesson the moral "Look first to the kingdom of God and all your material needs will be provided for." But we are seldom told *how* to look to God. For that, we must look carefully, not at what holy people say, but at what they do.

Once when Jesus was preaching in the countryside to a gathering of about five thousand men, women, and children, it got so late that the crowd could no longer travel home to fetch provisions. The disciples became worried that the people would have nothing to eat, and so they brought the problem before Jesus. "There is a lad here, which hath five barley loaves, and two small fishes," explained Andrew, "but what are they among so many?" (John 6:9).

Everyone knows the rest of the story. Jesus took the loaves and fishes and offered thanks to God, then commanded the twelve disciples to distribute them among the multitude—and all five thousand were fed. In the end, just to be certain that the disciples hadn't missed the lesson of the miracle, he commanded them to gather up the fragments left over from the meal, and it filled twelve baskets—the number of disciples who had doubted the multitudes could be fed.

So what does the holy person *do* in this story? Actually, there are two holy people to begin with—Jesus, and the lad who offers his loaves and fishes to the disciples—then more and more as the story progresses. A sermon I once heard explains the mystery of the miracle by offering an even greater miracle in its place. That version of the story goes something like this.

As the disciples went about asking if anyone had brought food, each person was careful to protect the bit of bread or fish he had brought along for himself and his family. "There isn't enough to share" must have been the thought in everyone's mind. But then the disciple Andrew came upon a young boy who, without any calculating thoughts of this kind, simply offered what he had. Jesus said it was sufficient, just as the belief of one person is often enough to inspire many, and as the baskets were being passed around, sure enough, the people began to bring out what food they had brought along and share it with their neighbors. No wonder there were twelve baskets left over. The version of the miracle that has Jesus simply multiplying the loaves and fishes is rather tame in comparison to the one in which what is multiplied by five thousand is the belief of a single child.

In the story of Elijah and the widow of Zarephath, again there are two holy people. God has sent the one to the other. But as for who is being fed, it isn't really clear. True, the widow offers food to Elijah, but through the miracle he performs, she is fed many times over. And so it's not clear whether God has sent Elijah to be fed by the widow, or to feed her. As always with God, there are more dimensions at work than we can comfortably handle, the human brain being limited to considering one thing at a time.

There is always enough in the universe. That seems to be the point of the story. The universe is based on lack only if we look at it from a selfish point of view. Whatever else it accomplishes in spiritual terms, from a purely practical standpoint belief in God helps to break that monopoly. It helps to ease the one-dimensional restrictions we place upon ourselves and the world.

Not long after we moved from Manhattan to Woodstock and I'd found another café to write in, I was sitting at my usual table next to the entrance when a man in his mid-fifties who looked vaguely homeless came up to the window and held up a public-library copy of one of my books. Pointing at the photograph inside the dust jacket and then to me, he raised his eyebrows interrogatively, and I nodded yes. I motioned him inside and, following a moment of hesitation in which he stole a furtive glance toward the manager's office, he steeled himself and slipped through the glass door to take the seat across from me. (I got the impression he wasn't normally allowed inside.)

He'd read the book, which had just come out, and wanted to tell me that he'd studied Buddhism under a Tibetan lama I had described as having a particularly keen understanding of young children. It occurred to me as I got to know Mark that this particular lama might have had a keen understanding of him as well, because, notwithstanding the fact that he'd once been a New York attorney, he was an innocent—one of those rare individuals who seem to get by in life like Jesus' lilies of the field.

He had lived since the mid-1960s behind the village green in a little unheated house that was always threatening to fall into the old mill stream, and by the time I arrived in Woodstock thirty years later he was a fixture of the town. Silent Mark, people called him, after his habit of going on "talk fasts" for indeterminate periods of time, although he was never silent with me. Quite the opposite. Often I couldn't shut him up, and had to break off our conversations midstream just to finish my shopping, or pick up the kids, or to get anything done at all.

Perdita developed a relationship with him as well. He saw the two of us together one day and apparently liked her at once, because after that he'd always find her whenever she was in town, even on her daily runs. He'd jog along beside her in his boots and sweater and baggy long pants, filling her in on local news—some plans for a new food co-op, a proposed development that would negatively impact the wetlands.

We were all poor at the time, though of course we weren't as poor as Mark. No one was, as far as I knew. But he never asked for money and wouldn't accept it when we offered. Probably he knew that we were writers struggling to make enough money just to pay the mortgage, and that sometimes we weren't even able to do that. Probably he knew a lot more than we gave him credit for at the time, or maybe he didn't. Maybe he just intuited something about the way the universe worked that we were only beginning to get a glimpse of at the time.

Once when we were counting pennies to get through the week, Perdita went to the grocery store with a carefully prepared list from which she'd struck through several items because we simply couldn't afford them. One was dishwasher detergent. It was that or milk, and so there was really no choice. But as she was walking back to the car with the groceries, Mark came up holding a jumbo-sized box of Cascade and said, "Here. Do you need this? Someone gave it to me, but I don't have a dish-washer." Coincidence? Or some kind of supermarket manifestation of universal compassion—it was impossible to tell. It happened so often, though, that when it did we used to just laugh and say, "Well, there he goes again!" I'd be looking for a particular religious text I'd once seen at a used book store years before and urgently needed for my writing but couldn't find anywhere, and Mark would appear one summer day, hand-ing it to me through the open car window in the middle of town. He'd got it for a quarter at the Woodstock Library Sale and thought I might be interested.

I think what really cinched it for us in the end was the sneakers. Be-fore that, the things he gave us, though uncanny, didn't really inspire us to believe. They seemed like some quirky kind of telepathy, or maybe a way of being in the universal groove—something that might as easily have been the psychic by-product of too many drugs during the 1960s as a manifestation of the Divine. But then one day Perdita was running past the village green and Mark came rushing up to her from the bench where he'd been sitting, holding a new pair of red Nike running shoes. "Here! You need these, don't you?" He'd found them at Family of Woodstock, the local relief organization that collected clothes for the poor.

Perdita was a little annoyed that she'd have to carry them for the re-maining two miles of her run, besides which there was little chance they'd fit. She has wide feet (courtesy of her Irish peasant ancestry, she always claims), and it was impossible to find shoes that fit. Only the most expen-sive ones would work, and there was no way we could afford to buy a new pair for her. The ones she was wearing had been repaired with duct tape, and she'd remarked more than once to me in the last week or so that she'd have to stop running soon, because her knees were giving out.

I knew what that meant. Family ecologies being what they are,

Perdita's daily run through Woodstock kept our household operating smoothly. In most families there is one person, usually, though not always, the mother, or grandmother, or an older sister, who makes the whole thing work—who takes care of everybody, and makes sure they're fed and bathed, that they keep their dentist appointments and have fresh clothes to put on in the morning. I participated, of course, had my regular responsibilities and chores, but as often as not I'd have to be told three or four times what to do, and Perdita did the telling. She had the whole thing set out like a flowchart inside her brain. But with a long-distance run taken out of the equation, the whole thing would quickly fall apart. And that's exactly what it was starting to do.

Of course, the sneakers fit perfectly. They were exactly Perdita's size—width and all—and she ended up wearing them for four and a half years, so long in fact that the kids took to calling them Mommy's Magic Shoes. And perhaps they were. Strange things happen when a person with nothing gives you something, and suddenly, together, you have everything. It's not the same as having enough to go around, or having surpluses. What is a surplus anyway but too much for the person who has it to use? "Blessed are the poor in spirit: for theirs is the kingdom of heaven," says Jesus in the Gospel of Matthew (5:3)—the very first words of his public ministry in the Bible. Later, in the Gospel of Luke, he says the same thing, only in this case there is no mention of the spirit. He says simply, "Blessed are the poor."

15

Elijah Prays for Rain

And Elijah went up to the top of Carmel; and he cast himself
down upon the earth, and put his face between his knees,
And said to his servant, Go up now, look toward the sea. And he
went up, and looked, and said, There is nothing. And he said,
Go again seven times. And it came to pass at the seventh time,
that he said, Behold, there ariseth a little cloud
out of the sea, like a man's hand.

—1 KINGS 18:42–44

Just as the Lord told Elijah at the beginning of his ministry that it would not rain for many years, now he is told that the drought is about to end. Elijah goes to King Ahab to tell him this and immediately ascends Mount Carmel to pray. There he sits with his face between his knees—the traditional posture of prophets when called on to wait before God. And that is what he does. He waits. His servant must think Elijah is crazy, sending him to the top of the mountain six times to look for something that isn't there. But then, on the seventh try, he sees the sign that Elijah has been waiting for—a cloud the size of a man's hand telling him that the drought is about to end.

When we first begin spiritual practice we usually aren't very good at this kind of waiting; we want something to happen right away. We look for a sign that we are getting the hang of it, that we are doing it right, or at least that we are on the proper path.

At the start, in fact, we often do receive just this kind of sign. God is indulgent with beginners, just as a parent is with a child. Using Elijah as the model, you might say that we need to be fed by ravens at first just to know that God is there. The farther we go on the path toward God, however, the less these signs appear. Think of it as a journey into the wilderness. As we leave our homes there are plenty of signs to mark our way. As we near the wild, however, such signs quickly diminish. For a while there are trail markers, then even these disappear and we are alone in nature, which is much like being alone with God.

As a child growing up in rural Arkansas, I knew a man who took the experience of waiting more seriously than anyone else I have known. Mr. Kelso worked for my grandmother as a kind of all-purpose handyman, looking after her rental properties and making occasional repairs to the home. At that time I was fatherless (my mother had divorced when I was born and had not yet remarried), and so, as Kelso seemed always to be involved in some activity having to do with tools or vehicles, very early I started to follow him about.

He had the appearance of a man who had spent the greater part of his life outdoors. He was slim but strong-looking. His hands and face had long since been given up to the sun. The rest was never visible, for even on the hottest, brightest days Kelso wore khakis and heavy boots and never rolled his sleeves. Only once, as he was making an adjustment to the outboard motor of the little fishing boat we took out every Saturday morning, did I have the opportunity, while standing behind him, to look down the back of his shirt. The skin was smooth and white, even young-looking, and for a long time afterward I felt vaguely ashamed, as though I had discovered a part of him that no one was ever meant to see.

He loved fishing, and here his manner gave the impression of a man who had spent long days alone on the water with no one for company but the sky. Most days he spoke little or not at all. We would putter about in the outboard making wrinkles on the glass body of Lake St. Francis, until finally we found a little cove where Kelso thought the bass might be biting that day. After that we would bait our hooks and set them. And that, as they say, was that.

I remember my Uncle Jimmy once remarking that Kelso unnerved the fish. The way he switched the motor off and just sat there for a full ten minutes before even setting his pole let them know how it would go. "Fish," explained Jimmy, "know right away what kind of man you are, and those fish knew Kelso could wait better'n God. Five, ten minutes like that and they'd be settin' their own mouths good and proper right there on the end of his line."

As a child I was a little in awe of Kelso, not just because he could take apart anything and put it back together better than it was before, but because of this ability to wait. There was a peacefulness that seemed to follow him through everything he did. It gave you the sense that there was no hurry, that all things would take their proper course if you were sensible, and patient, and trusted God to make them so. Looking back on those mornings alone on the water with Kelso, it seems I was learning more from him than just fishing. Though at the time all I wanted in life was to catch a really big bass.

The story of Elijah praying for rain is sometimes interpreted as a parable on prayer, the moral of which is "Go again seven times." It then becomes a lesson in persistence, similar in some ways to waiting with your pole in one place long enough for the fish to begin to bite. But there is a deeper lesson than that at the heart of the story. As always in the Bible, provided we have the patience to unravel them, we find that we are being taught many things at once.

The first thing to notice about the story is that the jobs of praying and watching are divided. They aren't done by the same person. Elijah remains in prayer, while his servant goes off to see what, if anything, has happened.

When we first begin to practice, we tend to watch for results. We look to see if the meditation is making us enlightened, if the prayer is getting answered. But trying to do both jobs at once reduces our practice to the level of brute mechanics. "If I do A," we tell ourselves, "then B ought to follow," and then we check to see if it is so. But that isn't how spiritual practice works. B doesn't follow from A, and A doesn't *cause* B—A and B are the same. That is what I meant earlier when I wrote that prayer is the *practice* of belief. It's really pointless trying to separate the two.

Naturally, this doesn't mean that we can avoid looking over our own shoulders to see how our spiritual journey is getting on. In spite of all our good intentions, and no matter how strong our resolve "to pray for prayer's sake," we will check up on ourselves from time to time because we are self-conscious beings—because in the beginning we don't trust God to take us wherever we need to go. For this reason, many people choose to work with a spiritual director—anyone from the local priest or rabbi to an older, more experienced "spiritual friend." That person's task is to take over the job of watching so that we can simply pray.

In a sense, the servant is just an extension of Elijah. After all, it's Elijah who keeps sending him back up the mountain. At the same time, Elijah doesn't go himself, but remains focused on his prayer. The lesson here is not to take stock of our practice *while* we are practicing, not to look to see if the prayer is working *while* we are engaged in prayer. That is the first lesson, and it is a very simple one: while we are praying, we should forget everything else and simply pray. Leave the looking to God, or to a spiritual director, or at least to some later moment in time.

As time goes on, we get better at this. We are able to practice for longer and longer periods without anxiously looking for a sign, with the result that, as the spiritual journey goes along, fewer signs appear. This is an indication that we have learned the art of waiting, that we have learned not just to believe in our practice, but to practice our belief. We sit down to pray and trust God to direct us, so we don't have to worry so much where it will go.

So that is the first lesson—learning to wait. But that is not where the story ends.

The first six times the servant goes to the top of Mount Carmel, he returns to Elijah and says, "There is nothing." On the seventh trip, however, at last he sees the cloud Elijah has been waiting for.

If we keep looking seven times—that is, if we make a practice of praying, instead of just occasionally saying a prayer or two—eventually something will appear out of that nothingness. And the way we know that that something is from God is that it appears on the other side of nothing. On our side, there are all our thoughts and feelings, hopes and fears, reflected, as it were, on the inner surface of the self. But eventually, if we keep at it long enough, those things will all disappear. At this point, even though there are no signs to mark the way, we are nevertheless called to walk forward, guided by the call of God.

Once a disciple came before the Baal Shem Tov, the founder of Hasidism, and said despairingly, "I try to draw close to God, but whenever I do God retreats from me, and I find myself getting no closer."

"And how did you teach *your* child to walk?" asked the Baal Shem Tov.

The disciple replied, "Well, by standing close, and then as he took a step, I would take a step back. And as he would take another step, I would take another step back, until one day he could walk."

"This is what God is doing with you," concluded the Baal Shem Tov.

We want a sign from God at the beginning of our spiritual journey, and in the beginning we usually get one. Then, as the journey proceeds, the signs become very few. Why is this so? Because that is how God teaches us to walk. Because that is how God teaches us what only God *can* teach us, and that is the practice of belief.

But even that is not quite all there is to the story. What about the cloud that appears from the other side of nothing? And why does it take the shape of a hand?

The cloud witnessed by Elijah's servant is very small—the tiniest cloud you could see, just like a little hand coming up over the horizon. So small is it, in fact, that it might almost seem insignificant, if it weren't for the fact that it is shaped like a hand. That makes it intimate, and that intimacy gives Elijah an intimation of things to come. When it pops up from below the blank horizon of the sea, immediately he leaps up.

> *And he said, Go up, say unto Ahab, Prepare thy chariot, and get thee down that the rain stop thee not. And it came to pass in the mean while, that the heaven was black with clouds and wind, and there was a great rain. And Ahab rode, and went to Jezreel. And the hand of the Lord was on Elijah; and he girded up his loins, and ran before Ahab to the entrance of Jezreel.*
>
> (1 KINGS 18:44–46)

A tiny cloud, the story tells us. But, really, it could be anything that gives us that tiny intimation of what is right, of what to do, or, in certain cases, even of what is to come. Here the story of spiritual practice is made into a dramatic narrative with characters who are larger than life. But this can and will happen to us as well if we learn to wait on God. If we actually do this practice, we'll find, often unexpectedly, that when we're facing some obstacle or having difficulty moving farther down the path, if we look past the thoughts and images in our mind, look past them to this nothingness, and then beyond that nothingness to the intimation, we will receive our inspiration or our answer. And that is how we find our way along on the spiritual journey.

God takes a step back and holds out his hand as if to say, "Come a little closer." We take a step. And God moves back again. And sometimes we have to stay with that for a while—not just seven times in most cases, but seventy times seven. The only thing certain is that, at some point, a little hand will appear, and embracing that little hand, that small intimation, we will feel ourselves drawn toward it and finally *into* it. It's as if God is drawing us toward him, pulling us farther in. At that point we are carried along, swept up by the wind of the spirit like Elijah, the hand of God upon him, running ahead of the rain.

16

A Still Small Voice

> And, behold, the Lord passed by, and a great and strong wind
> rent the mountains, and brake in pieces the rocks before the
> Lord; but the Lord was not in the wind: and after the wind
> an earthquake; but the Lord was not in the earthquake: And
> after the earthquake a fire; but the Lord was not in the fire:
> and after the fire a still small voice.
>
> **—1 KINGS 19:11–12**

When we draw close to God, everything happens . . . and nothing does. On the one hand, we may have what we feel to be an authentic experience of the Divine. We feel changed, transformed, born again. It seems as though everything about our lives, our way of understanding ourselves and our world, is permanently altered. On the other, we cannot possibly point to anything definitive about that encounter. Afterward, we can't say, "It was like this!" or "It was exactly like that!" God isn't *like* anything. And so we are left snatching at metaphors in the attempt to account for what has happened to us, to clothe the infinite in words, the unprecedented in terms of what we already know.

The beautiful thing about the Bible's description of Elijah's encounter with God is that it makes no attempt to do this. We are told that there was a great wind, but that God was not in the wind. We are told that there was a powerful earthquake, but that God was not in the earthquake. That there was fire, but God was not in that either. Then comes "a still small voice." We aren't told that God was *not* in it; nor are we told that he *was*—only that afterward Elijah went out to stand at the entrance of the cave with his cloak pulled up over his face.

A still small voice . . . Those words have been variously translated as "a light whisper," "a soft murmuring sound," and "a sound of sheer silence." I recently attended a gathering at which this verse became the subject of discussion. Together with an Orthodox Torah scholar and a woman who was studying to be a rabbi, we arrived at our own translation: "And after the fire the thinnest possible silence." Thin, as in hammered gold. Thin, as in the thinnest possible membrane. On one side stands Elijah, on the other God. No wonder when he steps outside the cave, he covers his face with his cloak.

There is a parallel story from Exodus, in which Moses begs God to be allowed to see his face. God tells Moses that no one shall see his face and live but that he will nevertheless cause his "glory" to pass before him. Instructing Moses to climb down inside the cleft in a rock, God places his hand over the top, removing it only at the last possible moment so that Moses can catch a glimpse of his retreating back. Jewish tradition has it that Horeb and Sinai are the same mountain, and, indeed, that the cave where Elijah spends the night is the very "cleft in the rock" where Moses hid so that he could witness the glory of the Lord without being obliterated.

God's back, but not his face.

There is a subtle wisdom here. We are not allowed to anticipate the Divine. It isn't like anything we know, not like anything we could even imagine in terms of what we know. We don't arrive at it by following the mind road to some very lofty, rarefied, or purified conception of God. We arrive by stepping beyond the mind altogether, by turning it, as it were, inside out, so that it no longer seeks to contain God in thought but rather casts itself *upon* God, or *into* God.

It is like casting a thimble upon the sea. A thimble can't hold very much of the sea. You can't scoop up a bit of the ocean in a thimble and say, "This is the ocean." But you can certainly toss it in. To toss a thimble into the ocean is, in a sense, to turn it inside out—so that it is contained by what it cannot contain. In the same way, we can't *know* God, but we can enter into a state of unknowing in which *we are known.* That is why the anonymous author of a fourteenth-century manual on contemplative prayer called his work *The Cloud of Unknowing*—he knew it was only possible to come to God by casting our thimble upon the sea.

And yet, the question is always the same: how do we *do* this? It's fine to contemplate a metaphor if that helps to inspire us. But what must we do to actually take those final steps past the entrance of the cave where we can be known by God?

There are as many methods of doing this as there are cultures and people to employ them, and no one holds the universal patent. Change the words being used, and any one of the practices that focus on the repetition of a holy name is essentially the same as any other, whether that name be Hindu, Buddhist, Jewish, Christian, Muslim, or something less familiar. All are ways to God. The same with meditation. Apart from the different objects of contemplation being employed, they are all ways of entering the conversation with God. We mustn't be fooled by talk of the breath, the chakras, or the various heavenly realms of this or that buddha or god. We personalize a particular way to God so that it suits our cultural circumstances and pronounce it "correct" or "right," but in the final analysis it is only right for *us*—and maybe a few others in our community. *All* are right for God.

All are right . . . and none of them are. Actually, there is no spiritual practice that reaches as far as God. At some point in the ongoing conversation of spiritual practice, when we have used up all our spin, when we have exhausted all our many stratagems for getting ourselves forgiven, or enlightened, or saved, there comes a call to step beyond. There is no way to rush that event. The lead-up to it takes as long as it takes, and it may take the better part of a lifetime, because God is patient and we are very stubborn, and there is a seemingly endless supply of wind in the world, not to mention earthquakes and fire. Nevertheless, somehow the moment always comes.

When the time comes for Elijah, he follows the call of God to the entrance of the cave and takes a step beyond. This is what we are all called to do. Without it there can be no lasting belief. We must follow God's call to the very edge of what we can know and understand (which is the same as saying "what we can control") and take a step beyond, surrendering to a Power Beyond the Self.

Finally, any spiritual practice must contain this one essential element of surrender. With it, God will lead the way—even if we feel completely lost, even if we aren't sure where we are going with it or what we are doing. Without it, we are apt to go astray, no matter what we do. In fact, we need little more than that to begin with, little more than the *willingness* to believe.

Once when Jesus was with his disciples Peter, James, and John (coincidentally, just following a vision during which they saw Jesus standing on a mountaintop between Moses and Elijah), they came upon a man with an epileptic son. The father asked Jesus to help him if he could, whereupon Jesus replied: "All things are possible to him who believes." "And straightway the father of the child cried out, and said with tears, Lord, I believe; help thou mine unbelief" (Mark 9:24). This is the model for anyone who takes up a spiritual practice. We would never do such a thing if we weren't already caught in the struggle between faith and doubt. A spiritual practice—*any* spiritual practice—is the expression of that struggle. Therefore, at the heart of all practice is the same simple plea: "Help thou my unbelief!"

That is why Elijah is in the cave in the first place. He has gone head-to-head with the most powerful political forces of his day, with the result that Queen Jezebel has now sworn to kill him before the setting of another sun. And so Elijah flees into the wilderness, finding his way over a period of forty days and forty nights back along the course Moses took to bring the Israelites to the Promised Land, until he comes to the mountains where Moses received the tablets of the law. There he hides himself in the cleft of the rock, nursing the most profound doubts about the future of his prophetic mission. When a voice speaks to him asking what he is doing hiding there instead of pursuing his mission in the world, Elijah answers, "The children of Israel have forsaken thy covenant, thrown down thine altars, and slain thy prophets with the sword; and I, even I only, am left; and they seek my life, to take it away" (1 Kings 19:10). That is when the voice tells him to go and stand at the mouth of the cave, the place of practice, the place we occupy to express our willingness to believe, whatever doubts might be assailing us at the time. And a great wind comes. Then an earthquake. Then a fire.

Finally "a still small voice" calls to Elijah and he steps forward out of the cave mouth. Whatever practice he has been doing (and although it must involve fasting, we're never told specifically what it is), at that moment it's over. All that remains is surrender. And there's really no practicing that.

"Lord, I believe; help thou mine unbelief." That about sums it up for us. We believe enough to find ourselves locked in the struggle between faith and doubt, but not enough to get ourselves clear of it. That isn't something we can do on our own. We can't toss our thimble, can't fall backward into the arms of God, until we believe in him, and we won't believe in God until he catches us when we fall. In the meantime, we have to do *something*—pray, meditate, say the rosary, even handle snakes or speak in tongues. We can't help it, and (however self-important people may feel about their religious practices) it doesn't matter so long as at the heart of it, implicit or spoken aloud, there lies a simple prayer for belief. If that is there, all else follows. God is waiting. And at some point (no one knows exactly how or why) we fall.

17

Questioning God

And the Lord said unto Satan, Hast thou considered my servant

Job, that there is none like him in the earth, a perfect and

an upright man, one that feareth God, and escheweth evil?

Then Satan answered the Lord, and said,

Doth Job fear God for nought?

—JOB 1:8-9

Job was once thought to be one of the oldest books in the Bible. We now know that it was composed much later. Nevertheless, the belief in its antiquity makes a certain kind of sense, because the question it addresses is the oldest one of all: why do we suffer?

The book of Job is an attempt to answer that fundamental question, and therefore its place in the Bible is an enigma in itself. Elsewhere the Bible maintains that God punishes sinners and rewards the just. Job alone seems a threat to that general assertion. Right in the middle of the Bible it appears out of nowhere, a forty-two-chapter discontinuity in the very fabric of Judeo-Christian belief.

As the drama opens, Job is cast as the unwitting pawn in a wager between immortals. Satan, in one of his few appearances in the Bible, returns to heaven for a reunion of the angels, whereupon God calls his attention to Job, a perfectly upright man who fears God and avoids all evil.

Satan is not impressed. "Does Job fear God for nought?" he replies, considering the fact that God has given Job a large family and caused him to prosper and protected everything he owns. "But put forth thine hand now, and touch all that he hath, and he will curse thee to thy face" (Job 1:11). And so, with God's permission, Satan goes forth to strip Job of all his possessions—his livestock, his servants, even his children.

Terrible as they are, Job answers these calamities with only the traditional expression of Jewish mourning: "The Lord gave, and the Lord hath taken away" (Job 1:21). And so next God allows Satan to go further and afflict his flesh and bone. Even Job's wife is no help to him at this point. "Curse God, and die," is the only advice she has (Job 2:9). It is here that the story of Job really begins. We find him reduced to nothing, seated on an ash heap, his body covered from head to foot with boils.

Directly three friends arrive to comfort Job, but in the beginning they don't know what to say. Clearly no consolation can begin to assuage his grief. Faced with the awful truth of Job's suffering, however, eventually they find their tongues, and each in turn does his best to explain it all away. If Job suffers, it must be because he has sinned. There *must* be something Job has done, or left *un*done, to explain what has happened; otherwise, the universe makes no sense. From their point of view, it matters little if, in the end, Job is innocent in his own mind. God must know something Job does not.

Despite the fact that a manual for liberation lies buried at the heart of it, for the most part the Bible is a document intended to promote and maintain certain norms of social and religious behavior. Therefore, the Bible's message generally seems to be "Play by the rules and God will protect you and make you prosper." But if we follow that line of thinking, it becomes easy to imagine that somehow we can "put a spin on God"— that we can understand God and manipulate him, and therefore assure our happiness and ultimate salvation by behaving in a certain way—which, paradoxically, would make *us* God, since it would give us a kind of power over him.

Job is a refutation of the idea that human beings can affect God in this way, by leaning one way or another on the moral scale, to the right or to the left—or even by keeping to the middle way. The simple truth is, what happens to Job happens to us all. Eventually we lose everything, whether we devote our lives to spiritual practice or not. The book of Job is only an accelerated version of the oldest and most universal human story: we are born and, if we are lucky, find love and grow old, but in the end, we lose everything, no matter what we do. There is no escaping the realities of old age, sickness, and death, even if we *could* say about ourselves what Job can, that we are perfectly good and righteous.

It is not surprising that for many people the book of Job calls into question the very nature of God—who he is, what he is, whether he's even good. And this itself is a kind of spiritual practice we can't avoid undertaking if we live and breathe in the world. It's part of the conversation with God. For some people it may be the biggest part of that conversation and therefore the greater part of their spiritual journey. For Job, it is everything. His practice before the story began was to be a good Jew, to play by the rules set forth by God (or simply by the religious authorities of his day). Once all that is over, however, and the illusion of spinning God with the body English of a blameless life has been demolished, all he has left is to question God.

But first he must learn *how* to question, because in the beginning he doesn't know. Questioning God isn't like asking questions of his friends. If Job wants to question God, he has to do so in a manner befitting the task. And that means asking a question that is big enough to contain the answer—an open-ended question. A question for which he has not secretly already prepared his own answer in advance.

This is what Shakyamuni Buddha did, coincidentally about the same time the book of Job was being composed. Faced with the inescapable reality of human suffering, he set out in search of an answer. Renouncing the comfort of the palace he had grown up in, he went to the forest and began to learn the various forms of spiritual practice available in his day. He mastered meditation, visualization, and renunciation, and fasted so well that eventually he was able to reach around the front of his body and grasp his backbone. But none of these methods worked. If anything, he only grew weaker and more despondent from practicing them.

Finally Shakyamuni accepted a bowl of rice and curds from a passing milkmaid and, with his strength restored, sat down under a pipal tree and resolved not to get up again until he had solved the problem of suffering—until he knew its ultimate source and the way beyond it.

That is where Satan enters the narrative. Mara, whose name means literally "murder and destruction," arrives to test the aspiring Buddha, threatening him with a vast army of demons, tempting him with visions of beautiful women, and so forth. But the Buddha remains seated beneath the pipal tree, gazing beyond the illusion of Mara's temptations to the very heart of the human condition, whereupon he finally cries out, "Oh, ignorance!"

About this moment, the Buddhist priest Akegarasu Haya wrote:

For a long time, I wanted to know Shakyamuni's exact thought at the moment of his awakening. But I could not understand it. Initially I thought that Shakyamuni awakened to his Buddha-nature. This was probably so, but I could hardly understand that within the context of my own life.

This year I have come to understand that Shakyamuni's exact thought at the moment of his awakening was expressed in his shout "Oh, ignorance!" "Oh, ignorance!" means "Oh, darkness!" When Shakyamuni said this, the devil whom he saw face to face was not

actually a devil in front of him, but was his own real self. . . . In
this sense, Shakyamuni's exact thought at the moment of his
awakening was his realization that "I am the devil."

"If he had shouted, 'Oh, light!' " Akegarasu concluded, "ignorance would have immediately appeared." In other words, the Buddha was able to become enlightened, not because he mastered meditation or understood God, but because he realized the true nature of the self. "Oh, ignorance!" he cries, and finds himself no longer Siddhartha, the person who thought he could pass beyond suffering by understanding it, but the Buddha, the Enlightened One who has relinquished for eternity all claims to self-importance and is simply "awake."

In the end, the question Job puts before God—"Why do I suffer?"— is made insignificant by the answer he receives in finding God. For find him he does. In chapter 38, God answers Job out of the whirlwind, saying: "Who is this that darkeneth counsel by words without knowledge? Gird up now thy loins like a man; for I will demand of thee, and answer thou me" (Job 38:2–3). It is, in every way possible, a reversal of roles. For the series of questions put to Job by God, containing some of the greatest mystical poetry ever written, has the ultimate effect of undoing not just the question, but the questioner himself. Which is another way of saying that Job's question, in being obliterated, is finally made big enough for God.

Imagine the answer the ocean might give to a sand grain that became concerned about the justice of its fate. Whatever answer a sand grain can have from the ocean must necessarily have the effect of making it feel, by comparison, unimaginably small. In fact, the Hebrew for the words "abhor myself," which Job uses in the last chapter of the book, derives from a root meaning "to melt into nothingness." Is it any wonder that, halfway through God's interrogation, Job says, "I will proceed no further" (Job 40:5) and claps his hand over his mouth?

In the end Job is vindicated and given back all that he had lost. In the final chapter God refers to him four times as "my servant Job," reaffirming what he stated about him at the beginning, that he is a perfect and an upright man. He even goes so far as to chasten Job's three friends for their remarks, for they have wronged not only Job (by attributing to him sins that he had not committed) but also God, about whom they "have not spoken of me the thing that is right, as my servant Job hath" (Job 42:7).

In the upshot, it seems clear enough that Job's friends believed it was possible to explain God, thus making his behavior morally comprehensible to man. That, then, is the thing that is wrong. But is this really any different from Job's attitude, because he too expected God to reward—or at least not punish—him for his good behavior? He, too, wants a God who is predictable and containable—a God he can influence and understand.

"The thing that is right" can only have been spoken by Job at the very end, when at last he comes face-to-face with God: *I have heard of thee by the hearing of the ear: but now mine eye seeth thee. Wherefore I abhor myself* [dwindle away to nothing], *and repent in dust and ashes*" (Job 42:5–6). Which is another way of saying that our nothingness is God's everything. And that is what it all comes down to in the end: a question that turns us inside out, an answer that reveals in the smallness of the sand grain the vastness and beauty of the sea from which it came—the sea that is always everywhere around it, and always has been and always will be. Forever and ever. Amen.

18

The Two Ways

For the Lord knoweth the way of the righteous:

but the way of the ungodly shall perish.

—PSALM 1:6

The Psalms are a Bible in miniature, a treasury of its deepest teachings. It's all there—every emotion, every insight, quite literally every possibility of human feeling and thought. In truth, we could study just the Psalms, or just the rest of the Bible, and in the end our understanding would be the same.

Within the Psalms themselves there is another treasury—a treasure *within* a treasure, which offers us valuable pointers on our way. For that reason, when the Psalms were first collected, it was put up front, in the place of honor, as a kind of introduction to all that followed. Its message was simple: there are two ways a person can take through life—the way of the righteous and that of the ungodly. The way of the righteous leads to happiness and prosperity; the way of the ungodly leads to death. Interpreted literally, the two ways are mutually exclusive. To follow one necessarily precludes following the other. Between them there can be no rapprochement, even until the end of time.

There is another way of interpreting Psalm 1 that is more liberating, however, because it does not lead to the "us versus them" mentality that has afflicted Western religion from its earliest days. In brief, it says that the Psalms were meant to be read internally, in the absence of projection. In other words, when the Psalmist speaks of enemies who "murmur against" him and "plot his destruction," the enemies he refers to are not literal enemies, but splintered-off aspects of the self, call them what you will—addictions, the shadow, or self-destructive thoughts, impulses, or deeds. Read this way, the psalm shows us that within our being there are both positive and negative potentials. We may choose to follow one or the other, and which one we choose will determine to a great extent our happiness or unhappiness in life.

But this does nothing to resolve the battle that rages all about us and within us, as well as throughout the Psalms and the Bible itself—that being the seemingly endless war between good and evil. It internalizes that war, to be sure, making it less risky for ourselves and our neighbors; but it doesn't actually stop it.

Fortunately, contained within Psalm 1, there is the secret of a "third way," a way that stops the war altogether, thus healing the split we experience internally and externally at nearly every level of ordinary life. Whereas the literal approach sees life as divided into two enemy camps, and the psychological approach (which embraces a more modern, liberal sensibility) sees it as composed of two parts that make a whole, the mystical approach sees a whole with no parts whatsoever, because it interprets the whole psalm as a practical instruction on prayer. How better to begin the Psalms, sometimes called the "prayer book of the Bible," than with a clear, simple teaching on how to pray?

The mystical teaching sees only the way of the righteous. The way of the ungodly is not real. Thus it "shall not stand in the judgment" (Psalm 1:5), but perishes at once in the light of God's truth. I am struck by how similar this approach is to the basic teaching of a book that for many people serves as a kind of substitute Bible. *A Course in Miracles* begins with its own short "psalm":

> *Nothing real can be threatened.*
> *Nothing unreal exists.*
> *Herein lies the peace of God.*

"For the Lord knoweth the way of the righteous: but the way of the ungodly shall perish." It perishes because "All is Other Power," because apart from the one true reality, which is God, nothing *can* exist.

According to Martin Buber, Rabbi Menahem Mendel of Kotzk once commented on the verse in the scriptures that reads: "Let the wicked forsake his way" (Isaiah 55:7).

"Does the wicked man *have* a way?" he asked and, when no one could reply, answered: "What he has is a *mire*, not a way. So what it meant is this: 'Let the wicked man leave his "way," that is, his illusion of having a way.'"

This illusion is perfectly illustrated in the first verse of Psalm 1:

> *Blessed is the man that walketh not in the counsel of the ungodly,*
> *nor standeth in the way of sinners,*
> *nor sitteth in the seat of the scornful.*

Notice the progression—from walking, to standing, to sitting. There is no "way" here in any active sense, only becoming gradually more and more stuck. It is understandable why the Kotzker rabbi described it as a mire.

The way of delusion starts off innocently enough—with our following the impeccably legitimate counsel of the worldly self, with its many concerns for our protection, security, and self-respect. But the price for that security is finally the spiritual journey itself, for eventually the search for God is abandoned altogether—whereupon we find ourselves seated among the "scoffers," those who say there was never any God to search for in the first place. But there is no need for projection here. What this really means is that finally we find ourselves "un-Godded"—in other words, hopeless and alone.

The way to avoid this fate is revealed in verse 2:

But his delight is in the law of the Lord;
and in his law doth he meditate day and night.

The word *law* has many meanings in the Bible, only one of which implies legality. Here it refers to the teachings, both in their written and internalized form. Thus, we are told that the blessed man is he who delights in the law of the Lord and "meditates" on it day and night—in other words, the person whose thoughts in each situation are primarily about God. Really, it is just that simple. The specific manner of thinking—and the practice, if any, associated with it—is less important.

Interestingly enough, the Hebrew word for "meditate," *hagah,* only means "to ponder, by muttering to oneself." This is a spiritual practice that lies within virtually anyone's capability, for it is something that everyone does constantly already, whether we hear them at it or not. This must have been the idea behind the opening scenes of Wim Wenders's remarkable film *Wings of Desire,* which portrays the work of angels in modern-day Berlin.

As the film opens we see people throughout the city in various situations, from the mortal to the mundane. Beside each one sits an angel, listening to his thoughts. Some are angry. Some worried. Some sad. One man kills himself. Another reads from the *Odyssey*. All are pondering their place in the world. And one or two are pondering God.

The overwhelming truth is—and this is what German poet Peter Handke must have had in mind in writing the script—*all are praying.* In 1 Thessalonians, Paul advises the first Christians to "pray without ceasing" (5:17), but we do this already. Why then are we not happy, or "blessed," as the psalm tells us we will be? It is because most of us experience that prayer only as talking to ourselves.

The simplest, and in many ways best, definition of prayer is "talking to God instead of only to oneself." Naturally, when you talk to someone else, you turn to face them, and that is what we must do in order to pray.

To face God means not to hide from God. It means to surrender our thoughts and feelings to him, to turn our being inside out so that those things that we call "me" or "mine" are instead called "thee" and "thine." As the psalmist says, "Trust in him at all times; ye people, pour out your heart before him" (Psalm 62:8). Naturally, this can work only if we don't hold anything back. Water poured out does not come back to the vase. So we pour it out . . . and let it go.

The most important thing to remember in this kind of prayer is that it does not ask us to judge our feelings and thoughts, only to surrender them. God will judge between truth and delusion, and the way of the righteous will emerge. We call it "the third way" because it stands above and apart from the battle between good and evil. It is a third way because it sets that battle to rest.

19

The Wakeful Heart

I sleep, but my heart waketh . . .

—SONG OF SOLOMON 5:2

The rabbi who taught me about Jewish prayer devoted several months to discussing one passage from the Mishnah, the code of Jewish law. In fact, it was all he ever discussed with me. He would walk over to the massive bookshelves that lined one whole wall of his living room, extract a large leather-bound volume, and, with no small show of ceremony, lay it open before us on the table, holding his beard out of the way with one hand, while with the other he bent forward, tracing the Hebrew letters with his forefinger until he found the passage in question. I expected him to go through the prayer book, explaining the She'ma ("Hear, O Israel, the Lord our God, the Lord is One"), the Eighteen Benedictions, and the various other cornerstones of Jewish liturgy. Instead, he took down the very same volume each week and began by reading the same passage: "Do not stand to pray except with a heavy head. The first Hasidim would wait an hour and then pray, in order to direct their hearts to their father in the heavens" (Berakoth 5:1). Then he would ask, "Why did the ancient rabbis say, 'Do not stand to pray except with a heavy head'?"

When I asked this same question at our Thursday night Bible study meeting, one of the members said something I have never forgotten. She observed that when a child begins to grow in its mother's womb, its body forms a circle, so its head actually touches its heart. As time goes on, however, the head gradually comes up and the body grows straight, so that by the time the child is born, that is no longer possible. We keep our heads up, looking about us at the world, captivated by all we see, and eventually the heart is all but forgotten. In order for the head to touch the heart again, she explained, it must be allowed to grow heavy. "And that's the whole spiritual journey," she concluded. "It covers just that short distance from the head to the heart, no more—and yet, look how much trouble it causes us!"

When we begin the practice of prayer, it seems that the heart lies at a great distance from us. Sometimes we have strayed so far, in fact, that we no longer even remember in which direction it lies. But, in reality, to travel that distance only requires a heavy head. Physically speaking, whether we are standing or sitting, the head lies on a plumb line with the heart—if it "falls" there is no place else for it to go.

Although today many of us are engaged in a spiritual practice of one form or another, we seldom consciously experience what the ancient rabbis called "a heavy head." Nevertheless, that experience revisits us all at least once daily as we fall asleep. Our heads grow heavy . . . and we nod off. It isn't the same as standing to pray after an hour of turning our hearts toward God, and in the morning we have little recollection that anything has happened. But it's a good place to start in our recovery of the ancient art of prayer.

After only three weeks of following a "prehistoric schedule" of sleep, the participants in a study at the National Institutes of Health said they had never known what it felt like to be awake. Researcher Thomas Wehr had asked his subjects to follow a sleep schedule based on a midwinter night fourteen hours in duration, retiring at darkness and rising with the light. He wanted to determine if modern human beings had preserved something like a natural time clock that kept their ratio of sleep to waking calibrated to the seasonal changes in light.

They had.

Given the chance, the participants—all ordinary men and women like ourselves—reverted to what Wehr concluded must have been the earliest human mode of winter sleep: they began each night by lying quietly in bed for two hours in a resting state that Wehr describes as neither wakefulness nor sleep, but another state "with an endocrinology all its own." They then slept for four hours before waking for another two hours of "rest," after which the pattern began again.

"It is tempting to speculate," wrote Wehr, "that in prehistoric times this arrangement provided a channel of communication between dreams and waking life that has gradually been closed off as humans have compressed and consolidated their sleep."

In speculating about life prior to the invention of the electric lightbulb, the Jesuit historian John Staudenmaier reached a similar conclusion:

> *Activities that need good light—where sharp tools are wielded*
> *or sharply defined boundaries maintained: purposeful activities*
> *designed to achieve specific goals; in short, that which we call*
> *work—all this subsided in the dim light of evening. Absent the*
> *press of work, people typically took themselves to home and*
> *were left with time in the evening for less urgent and more*
> *sensual matters: storytelling, sex, prayer, sleep, dreaming.*

It is interesting to note that, of the "more sensual matters" mentioned by Staudenmaier, all except sleep itself involve communication—with one another, with God, with that deeper aspect of the self we call the "heart" or "soul."

What does it mean that we no longer make the space to commune with our hearts? And what would happen if we made that space again?

The problem is that we have redefined wakefulness in the modern world in such a way that it excludes the experience of a wakeful heart. By "being awake," today we mean something closer to the ability to perform the kinds of activities Staudenmaier described as "needing good light." Driving a car, for instance. Driving requires the kind of wakeful reflexes we need to get us where we need to go, but not the kind of wakefulness that tells us if where we are headed is where we ought to be going in the first place. It doesn't provide us with a sense of meaning, or connection, or a sense of purpose in living in the world. If anything, that kind of wakefulness—generated from without by artificial light, by caffeine, by tasks requiring a tense, focused consciousness rather than a supple, relaxed one—tends to distract us for long intervals from the purpose of our days.

It is almost as if, in the modern world, the diurnal rhythms of consciousness themselves have been inverted, so that the part of us that was supposed to remain ever wakeful is allowed to slumber, while the part that ought to be given rest has had its eyelids permanently pried wide open and given the reins over life. No wonder things are so out of control.

"I sleep, but my heart waketh . . ." The verse is taken from the Song of Solomon, a lyrical love poem that is unique among all the books of the Bible in its joyous portrayal of sexual love, unique as well in that, apart from Esther, it is the only book that never mentions the name of God. For both reasons, perhaps, its inclusion in the Hebrew canon was once the subject of great debate. Eventually the love of poetry prevailed—that and the fact that many of the ancient rabbis insisted it was really a manual of prayer. They weren't shocked that the author had portrayed prayer as a love affair with God. The erotic images and the drowsy love talk of the Song accorded quite well with the intimacy they experienced in their nightly conversation with God. "I sleep, but my heart waketh" describes perfectly the moment when our hearts enter that space between dreaming and waking, familiar to all lovers as well, when praying becomes as easy as breathing, the flow of words issuing unimpeded and unguarded from our lips. The heart is the only witness to what passes in that conversation. The head wakes up at some point much further along on the spiritual journey, with only the sense that something momentous has occurred.

That is why my rabbi friend never discussed with me the intricacies of Jewish prayer. He knew it was enough to teach me to rest my head on God's shoulder like a lover. He wasn't concerned with what specifically ought to be said. Like lovers, when the moment comes, we know.

20

Jonah and the Vine

And God said to Jonah, Doest thou well to be angry for the gourd? And he said, I do well to be angry, even unto death.

—JONAH 4:9

Jonah, the most reluctant prophet in the Bible, is ironically also the most successful. He preaches to the people of "that great city Nineveh," and everyone—from the king himself down to the animals—immediately dons sackcloth and begins to fast. It's as if the repentance of the Ninevites, ostensibly the main action of the story, were really a kind of subplot. And, in fact, that seems to be the case. The story isn't really about the Ninevites, whom God could save just as easily on his own. It's about Jonah, who doesn't want them to be saved and is therefore in danger of losing salvation himself. The real action of the story concerns God's attempts to save Jonah, who at one point confesses quite bluntly that if that means also saving the Ninevites, he'd rather die!

From the beginning, Jonah seems committed to the idea that Nineveh, that great enemy of the Jews, ought to be destroyed. The reason for his anger in the story, and for the fact that initially he flees his mission, only to be swallowed up by a great fish and brought back on course again, is that he can't live with the idea that he might actually become the agent of their deliverance. But it quickly becomes apparent that God intends to save the two together—the city and the prophet sent to prophesy against it, even if he is profoundly reluctant to be saved. That is what Jonah means when he tells God that he is "angry, even unto death." He would rather die than include his enemy in God's plan of salvation. He'd rather die than include the Ninevites in his prayer.

When we first moved to Woodstock, I was still running a poetry group in Manhattan. And so one night a month I found myself driving home very late at night, sometimes fighting to stay awake at the wheel. At first coffee worked well enough to keep me alert, but then I wasn't able to fall asleep for hours once I got home, and so to keep my mind sharp eventually I devised a game involving Christian radio. I called it "Waiting for the Other Shoe to Drop."

I'd begin each game by surfing the dial until I found a radio minister I liked. This wasn't as hard as some people might think. I'd grown up around plenty of God-fearing folk, and while I might not have liked their politics in some cases, the people themselves were often quite genuine. When I found a preacher who reminded me of the best Christians I'd known growing up, I would listen for a while to what he had to say about this or that passage from the Bible. Much of what I know about the Bible I learned that way. But in the end there nearly always came a "Jonah moment," where Christian charity reached its end. Some nights it would be homosexuality that would set off a tantrum of intolerance, or sometimes merely gender. On one occasion, a woman had called in to ask advice and was counseled quite sensibly on all manner of family and substance-abuse issues for half an hour before the minister in question became apoplectic over the fact that she had attended a service the week before where a woman had been allowed to preach. "But I suffer not a woman to teach, nor to usurp authority over the man, but to be in silence," he shouted, quoting the Apostle Paul. "For Adam was first formed, then Eve" (1 Timothy 2:12–13).

In fact, we all suffer moments like this, the desire to exclude *someone* from our prayers being universal to all human beings. Christian radio is only one example. We could find the same attitude, no doubt, on Muslim or Jewish radio—even on Buddhist radio, if there is such a thing. And not only there. In the wake of violent acts by foreign or domestic extremists, for an increasing number of people today, religion itself has become a kind of Nineveh that, from their point of view, the world could just as easily do without. And so it often happens that even religious persons may find themselves excluded from somebody else's prayer—even if it is only a secular or scientific prayer. The desire to exclude others is very, very strong.

We suffer from a seemingly terminal form of sibling rivalry where the grace of God is concerned. We want more of it than our brothers or sisters, and sometimes we want it all—as if salvation were a commodity that could be limited in such a way. As if it were a fixed resource that needed to be monopolized by Hindus or Buddhists, or by Muslims, Christians, or Jews. But, of course, if we could monopolize salvation in such a way, it would not *be* salvation. And God would not be God.

Next to Job, Jonah is the book of the Bible that contains the most heated conversation with God. It is the book in which the participants in that conversation most reveal themselves for who they really are. Jonah shows God what he really feels and thinks, holding back nothing, not even hatred, anger, and blame. And God, more intimate here than anywhere else in the Bible, listens patiently, taking it all in, always bringing the conversation back to the same simple question: "Do you have any right to be angry?"

At first Jonah doesn't answer. Instead, he builds a booth to the east of the city, hoping for a front-row seat at the apocalypse in the event the Ninevites' repentance is not enough to satisfy God. But God, for his part, proves loving toward both the Ninevites *and* Jonah, causing a gourd vine to grow up "that it might be a shadow over his head, to deliver him from his grief" (Jonah 4:6).

This alone should be enough to teach Jonah what he needs to learn, but it isn't. Jonah feels entitled to the vine. He feels he has a special right to be shielded from suffering, whereas the Ninevites do not. And so the next morning God tries another tack. He sends a worm to kill the vine and, when Jonah protests, asks again, "Doest thou well to be angry for the gourd?" To which Jonah replies, "I do well to be angry, even unto death" (Jonah 4:9).

In the upshot, we are *all* angry enough to die. And it is always anger that kills us. The lesson of Jonah is finally very simple: what destroys us is belief in the self, and *only* in the self. All creeds and catechisms notwithstanding, to believe in God is nothing more than to relax the claims of self-assertion long enough to realize that love is the one reality, a love that, in surpassing all the petty claims on existence by the self, embraces *all* beings equally as its sons and daughters. As Thomas Merton once wrote, no doubt paraphrasing Julian of Norwich, "Mercy upon mercy—all is mercy." Whether we call that mercy God or Vishnu or the universal ground of being makes no difference whatsoever. To assert one of these over another is always to choose anger over love.

And yet, it isn't Jonah's refusal to love the Ninevites that is the cause of his spiritual disease. (Given that we are creatures of preference, it is unavoidable to love the gourd vine and not the worm.) Rather, it is his failure to accept that all beings everywhere are the object of *divine* love. All moral failures are failures to recognize this one simple truth. No human wisdom extends beyond it, and anything that falls short of it is not yet wise.

Near the end of his book *The Loving Search for God: Contemplative Prayer and the Cloud of Unknowing,* the Trappist monk William Meninger wrote about his practice of taking twenty minutes each day to pray the Lord's Prayer, dwelling briefly on the significance of each phrase . . . "Thy kingdom come" . . . "Thy will be done" . . . "On earth as it is in Heaven" . . . In the beginning, Meninger was able to complete the whole prayer in one twenty-minute period, but as time went on that was no longer possible. Eventually, he was unable to get past even the opening words, "Our Father."

> *When we pray to our Father, we pray together with every man,*
> *woman, and child on the face of the earth. . . . This means that*
> *we may never exclude anyone from our prayer. When we say*
> *"Our Father" we put our arms around the shoulders of every*
> *one of God's children—barring none!*

It is easy to understand why Meninger found it difficult to get past the opening words of the prayer—the entire teaching of Jesus is contained within them. That teaching isn't something we can get around or get past in order to go on to bigger and better things. It is already the biggest, best thing there is. And yet how hard it is for us to embrace that vision. How many of us, in praying the Lord's Prayer, can honestly claim that we have embraced even the first word of it?

In the end, all failures of belief or practice are failures to include all beings in our prayer. We cannot pray without them, for in so doing the one we pray to is not God but ourselves. For God to be God, he must be the God of all beings everywhere. Thus, in the end God says to Jonah: "Thou hast had pity on the gourd, for the which thou hast not labored, neither madest it grow; which came up in a night, and perished in a night: And should not I spare Nineveh, that great city, wherein are more than sixscore thousand persons that cannot discern between their right hand and their left hand; and also much cattle?" (Jonah 4:9–11).

If Jonah has an answer for God, the Bible doesn't tell us what it is, because that is where the story ends—with the vision of a world in which we have no right to be angry for the mercy God offers to us all.

Revolution

21

Jesus Holds Up a Flower

Consider the lilies of the field, how they grow;

they toil not, neither do they spin . . .

—MATTHEW 6:28

On the central wall of the guesthouse at the monastery where I lived during the 1980s, there was a mural painted by the Japanese Jesuit priest Father Maxima depicting a scene from Buddhist legend. Once when Shakyamuni's disciples had gathered on Vulture Peak to hear a sermon, he simply stood in their midst and, holding a single flower aloft so all could see, twirled it between his thumb and forefinger. At this, all were puzzled. Mahakashyapa alone, among all the disciples, broke into a smile, indicating that he had understood the final truth of Buddhism.

Father Maxima's mural was a faithful depiction of all this. At the center stood Buddha holding up a lotus blossom. About him were the various monks and animals, along with the bodhisattvas, devas, and other heavenly beings normally to be found when Shakyamuni delivered a sermon. But Mahakashyapa wasn't smiling—at least it didn't look like any smile I'd ever seen. Rather, he wore an expression approaching horror.

Needless to say, I found this disturbing. I'd always believed that the gentle smile you saw on the faces of most Buddha statues was where I was headed in studying Zen. I didn't want the kind of smile Mahakashyapa had. In fact, I was a little afraid of it. When my turn came to clean the guesthouse, I'd always avoid the mural, working with my back to it, and when some visitor would ask to have the story explained, I'd recite it from rote without dwelling too much on the part about the smile. Even so, I'd often hear someone murmur behind my back as we turned to continue the tour, "Doesn't look like much of a smile to me!"

I finally asked the abbot about it, but all he said was, "Father Maxima got it right."

When Jesus first opens his mouth to teach in the New Testament, it is clear at once that "he gets it right" and, consequently, that we are in for a rocky ride. Because as loving and inclusive as his teachings are, they are completely uncompromising when it comes to the worldly concerns of the self.

Nowhere is this more apparent than in the Sermon on the Mount, when he counsels his disciples not to worry about the things that normally occupy people's minds:

> And why take ye thought for raiment? Consider the lilies of the
> field, how they grow; they toil not, neither do they spin: And yet I
> say unto you, That even Solomon in all his glory was not arrayed
> like one of these. Wherefore, if God so clothe the grass of the field,
> which to day is, and to morrow is cast into the oven, shall he not
> much more clothe you, O ye of little faith?
>
> (MATTHEW 6:28–30)

On its surface, Jesus seems to be saying we ought to trust in God to provide for us at every moment of our lives—that if God cares so well for all the rest of nature, he will surely care for us. But at the heart of that teaching lies a far more radical revelation that, if we truly embrace it, eliminates suffering altogether, because it removes the *cause* of suffering—because it goes back to the moment when, through an act of self-assertion, we first came to see ourselves as separate from God.

The simple fact is, no one feels able to live like a flower. Flowers don't pay mortgages on the fields where they live, don't have to worry about their jobs, their pensions, their children, or their health. Even when it's hot and doesn't rain for a long time, flowers never worry. They are born without worldly cares, and live and die in like manner. Flowers are at ease in the universe, even without thinking or trying at all. Over the centuries they have witnessed the fall of Troy, the death of Jesus, the bubonic plague, and the fall of the World Trade Center—all without missing a single pulse of the universal heartbeat. Their attentions never wander, they never become lost in the world. No wonder they look better than Solomon in all his fine robes. Dress yourself up any way you like—in Armani, Brooks Brothers, or Ralph Lauren—and it doesn't change for an instant what you are underneath: naked and fearful of what the next moment will bring.

When Jesus points to the lilies of the field—flowers that are born in a day and die in a day and never depart from the presence of God—he is not telling his disciples to *live* like them (which for most would be impossible), but that they *are* like them. That however much they worry, or puff themselves up, or tell themselves in a million and one little ways every day that it isn't so, they are one with all of creation. How could it be any other way?

This is the meaning of Shakyamuni's flower, and the reason why in Father Maxima's mural Mahakashyapa's mouth falls open in horror when he sees it. He knows at once the meaninglessness of individual selfhood, the pointlessness of all human enterprise and endeavor in the face of final annihilation. But then why at the end of the story does Shakya-muni say to those assembled, "The mind of true enlightenment I now pass on to Mahakashyapa"? Could that really be all there is? Is what many Christians say about Buddhism true, that it is a fundamentally nihilistic and pessimistic religion—which is to say, that it isn't really a religion at all?

No. What Shakyamuni understands is that the death of the self is al-ways followed by the birth of God. He has experienced this for himself and therefore knows that Mahakashyapa's enlightenment is assured. Had Father Maxima painted Mahakashyapa on any subsequent day, he would have shown the same smile the Buddha wore, but being a Christian, he chose to depict the moment *before* that smile, the moment he reaches the end of separate selfhood. The smile is left to God.

The first thing to realize on the spiritual journey is that we did not cause ourselves to be. The second is that over the course of our lives—whether they last for a day or a century—we are supported by a Power Beyond the Self that takes the form of everything from the earth we stand on to food and water, to sunlight, to the very air we breathe. We cannot live for even one day apart from these blessings, and yet we also don't cause *them* to be. Last of all, we need to know that we cannot catch our-selves when we fall—that in death we must surrender the self and all that we have made of it (or failed to make), entrusting everything, including all our thoughts, to the loving arms of God. But really, these three real-izations are all contained in a flower. Look at a flower and you have learned the complete teachings of the Buddha. Consider the lilies, and you have heard the entire Sermon on the Mount.

To understand the true meaning of salvation is to endure a spiritual death wherein we confront the inevitable and wholly unadorned fact of our common mortality. It is to understand, once and for all, that all be-ings, ourselves included, are flowers of the field and cannot be otherwise.

However urgently we seek to distinguish ourselves from one another and from the rest of nature, finding in our humanity the pinnacle of all creation, the simplest and most basic of existential facts is this: we exist on a level with all other beings—in the end we die the same death as the beetle or the rose.

The central question of the spiritual life then is this: what lies beyond the death of the self? How is it that Jesus sees living like the lilies of the field as the culmination of the spiritual life? How does it redeem us? How does it liberate us? How does it set our hearts at ease?

The Bible's answer to those questions is Jesus himself, whose name means literally, "The Lord Saves." Jesus' birth, his life and teaching, and his death are a flower held aloft by God that all might see. That is why through the ages so many Christians, mystics as well as ordinary men and women, both inside and outside the church, devout and heretic alike, have come to the life of peace with Jesus' name upon their lips. Jesus, whose name itself means "Other Power." Jesus, who embodies the teaching of entrusting to a Power Beyond the Self. No wonder devout Christians refuse to hear him equated with Thoreau, Gandhi, and Martin Luther King Jr. as merely a great spiritual leader. Even the comparison to Buddha in most cases offends them, but only because they do not yet understand that Buddha himself is more than just a man.

So how is it that Jesus saves us, liberates us, and sets our hearts at ease?

To understand the answer to these questions, first we have to understand how Jesus does *not* bring peace. Jesus does *not* bring peace to those who would use his name to assert the self. He does *not* bring peace to those who wear his name as a badge of privilege, or wave it as a banner justifying greed, oppression, or war. Nor does he still the hearts of those who use it like a first-class express ticket to the kingdom of heaven. In short, the name of Jesus does not bring peace to anyone who uses it to mean its opposite—to mean "I Save," or "My Church Saves," or "My Moral Behavior Saves." It should go without saying that he does not bring peace to the person who says, "I Am Saved by My Belief in Jesus Rather Than Allah, Buddha, Vishnu, or the Tao."

"I am the way, the truth, and the life: no man cometh unto the Father, but by me," says Jesus in the Gospel of John (14:6), but by that he doesn't mean that Muslim, Hindu, Buddhist, or even Jewish claims to the truth are invalid. As a Jewish rabbi, Jesus would have been familiar with the book of Proverbs, in which Wisdom, personified as a woman, says: "The Lord possessed me in the beginning of his way, before his works of old. I was set up from everlasting, from the beginning, or ever the earth was . . . whoso findeth me findeth life" (Proverbs 8:22–23, 35). This is the "I" Jesus refers to in John—the same "I" he uses earlier, when he tells the Pharisees, "Before Abraham was, I am!"

What distinguished Jesus from other Jewish teachers of the age was that he spoke directly out of that primordial wisdom as its embodiment, or *incarnation*. "No man cometh unto the Father but by me," Jesus said. And that is absolutely true—no one ever reached the Absolute except by following the path of transcendent wisdom. Buddha called it *prajna*, Lao Tzu named it *Tao*. Oddly enough, in the Zen tradition, it is known by the same name Jesus used: "the Way."

Jesus chose to embody wisdom and in so doing dared to live what others had only taught. He understood that in all the world there is only one way, and all of us are on it. No one is left behind.

Jesus does not privilege himself above a flower. His life and death, his actions and his teaching, even his name itself, attest to the fact that God saves those who cannot save themselves. That is why Jesus shows such love for the humble and the unassertive, for those who, far from being convinced of their own righteousness, are profoundly aware of the limits of their own power, and even of their capacity for good. The name *Jesus* itself is a testament to what he taught: that at the moment we relax the claims of self, even for an instant, and entrust ourselves as simply as a lily, we find that God's kingdom has already come. The moment of nakedness just before that "true entrusting" is a deeply terrifying thing, and there is no sin we human beings will not commit to avoid it—even in the name of religion. The moment after is another matter. A moment later, we are clothed again, but not in a fig leaf or in the hastily reassembled outfit we wore before. God clothes us in his smile.

22

The Evil Person

For everyone who exalts himself will be humbled,

and he who humbles himself will be exalted.

—LUKE 18:14*

If there is such a thing as the Islamic hell, then I am bound for it. I don't say this frivolously. I am not speaking tongue in cheek, as a person who'd just as soon go to the Islamic hell as the Christian heaven, because he doesn't believe that either one is real. I have no knowledge about what happens after death. I believe in the kingdom of God, which was, is, and shall be, but I don't know what form that takes in the hereafter—it's too big a thought for me. That I leave to God. About the Islamic hell, however, of one thing I'm certain. If it's real, I'm headed there—just as surely as the Islamic terrorists who destroyed the World Trade Center are now in the Christian hell (provided it too is real).

This was the conclusion I finally came to on the night of September

---

*New International Version.

11, 2001. I'd lived in Manhattan for ten years, celebrated Christmas dinner with my family on more than one occasion at Windows on the World, and actually worked in the Trade Center for a period of time, so the sense of loss was visceral. Later that day, when I was cleaning up toys the kids had left on the floor, I found a small plastic television set that had come with my daughter's dollhouse. Covering the screen was a tiny decal depicting the lower Manhattan skyline with the Twin Towers at its center. I stood there with it in my hand for what must have been a full five minutes before hiding it at the back of one of the kitchen drawers. The kids wouldn't miss it with everything else that was going on, and I didn't want them to see it. I had a hard time looking at it myself.

But later that night, unable to sleep, I went back down to the kitchen and took it out of the drawer. I took it into the living room and placed it at the feet of the medieval statue that rests on our mantle—a statue of Mary with her head tilted to one side, gazing lovingly at a small round object cradled in her palm. The woman I'd bought it from years before had told me it was the world. That was when I accepted my place in the hell of Islam. As long as the Mother of God was holding the world, I could trust in the way things played out. I could go wherever I had to go.

If there is anyone keeping track of the sins we commit against one another in the name of the self—whether by "self" we speak personally or in that collective sense we call a country, a religion, or a tribe—then we are *all* in trouble. Every American is in trouble, if for no other reason than the fact that Americans consume at least 25 percent of the world's resources but account for less than 5 percent of its population. But no one is immune to this kind of trouble. In general, the poor are a little better off, having less power and thus fewer opportunities to abuse it. But then the poor have sins of their own to contend with, even if most of them come from being poor. No one is immune.

Last year I traveled to Japan to meet with the leadership of Soka

Gakkai International, a lay Buddhist organization with members all over the world. One of these leaders, the man in charge of overseeing the monthly study meetings of the organization's twelve million members, told me about a trip he'd made the year before to meet with European Buddhists. "Even though they weren't Jews or Christians anymore, they had such a powerful awareness of original sin that it was difficult to talk with them about Buddhism."

"Did you tell them that original sin was karma?" I asked.

The conversation became much more interesting after that. Like many Christians, he'd always believed that original sin was some kind of curse people lived under, a state of "fallenness" from which it was impossible to recover. He'd never considered the possibility that it was the very web of cause and effect in which all created beings are caught, and from which they can never escape as long as they are alive.

Karma, of course, just means "deed." But as a religious teaching common in one form or another to most of the world's religions, it means something closer to the law of cause and effect. It is our link from one moment to the next, or—to put it in slightly more informal terms—the fact that one thing leads to another . . . and to another . . . and to another . . . ad infinitum. There is no definitive starting point for karma, and there is no end in sight. We are born into a sea of karma and depart from a sea of karma that is far more vast and complex than anything we could possibly imagine, because no one but God can see it whole. We never know the end of it—we don't even know the *beginning.* Thus, we can't point to any one evil deed and say, "This—and *just* this—caused such and such a set of consequences." What about *before*? What caused *that* cause? Once we start asking that kind of question, there is no end to it. We are all interrelated, all connected in the most unfathomable and unexpected ways by that net of "deeds." We call some of those deeds good and others evil, but God alone knows how it all fits together. Science can help us unravel the laws of cause and effect as they relate to the physical world (albeit to a very small part of it in comparison with the whole), but who can fathom the true depth of good or evil? Not you. Not me. Not anyone.

But then, how do we live with this sense of right and wrong we seem to have been born with, this weight of evil, or just plain suffering, that seems to weigh upon the world with such force that we must come up with a special name for it—original sin? How do we cope with karma, nothing but karma, as far as the eye can see?

The world itself is karma. It works according to the laws of karma, and so as long as we are in it, that is the name of the game. But there is no winning that game. There is no set of religious rules we can play by in order to come out on top. On top of *what*? The spiritual point of existence cannot be to come out on top of other beings, to prevail over them, or best them, or—in the event these prove impossible—simply to leave them out. In any case, karma makes this impossible. We are all too deeply interrelated for that. The only true salvation comes from recognizing this—that we are made to exist by a Power Beyond the Self, a power that pervades all things, working in so many dimensions at once, that with our limited senses we could never so much as begin to sort the whole thing out, much less spin it in our direction in order to come out on top. For God there is no top, there is no bottom. His love knows no direction, good or evil, up or down. We invented all that ourselves.

By far the most popular spiritual text in modern-day Japan, beloved by Christians and Buddhists alike, is a thirteenth-century religious treatise by the Pure Land saint Shinran called the *Tannisho*, or "Text Lamenting the Heresies." But what a strange little book it is, because each of the "heresies" it addresses is, in reality, some aspect of ordinary religious belief. In other words, what it considers heresy is what the ordinary person calls religion itself.

The most striking example comes at the beginning of Chapter 3:

"Even the good person attains birth in the Pure Land, how much more so the evil person." The first half of this expression is easy enough to understand. It means what most people already believe: that the good person goes to heaven. And, of course, that is absolutely true in the sense of his being saved. The person who abides by the norms of established religion will experience a salvation beyond his calculated bargain with Buddha or with God, a salvation which is necessarily more than he intended because it ultimately swallows up even his individual efforts at goodness, reducing them to irrelevance in the larger scheme of things. But then the second half says, "How much more so the *evil* person." Does this mean that the person who finds himself unable to live a good or moral life in his own eyes, but must turn to God for his deliverance, is even *more* saved? Not at all. *Both* are saved. Only, the evil person—lacking the self-righteous attitude of religious piety—is perhaps in a better position to experience such radical grace. For it only stands to reason, if *he* is saved, then the good person must be, too. For this reason, in the end it came to be said that Shinran's teaching consisted of the belief that the Buddha saves the evil person first.

This is the same teaching offered by Jesus in the Gospel of Luke:

Two men went up to the temple to pray; one a Pharisee, and the other a publican. The Pharisee stood and prayed thus with himself, God, I thank thee, that I am not like other men are, extortioners, unjust, adulterers, or even as this publican. I fast twice a week, I give tithes of all that I possess. And the publican, standing afar off, would not lift up so much as his eyes unto heaven, but smote upon his breast, saying, God be merciful to me a sinner. I tell you, this man went down to his house justified rather than the other: for every one that exalteth himself shall be abased; and he that humbleth himself shall be exalted.

(LUKE 18:10–14)

In reading this story, we may feel tempted to say that the one is saved but not the other. But Jesus' final comment exposes that lie: the person who exalts himself (the "good" person) will ultimately be humbled (become the "evil" person), whereupon he too will be exalted by God.

Such calculated effort as that shown by "the good person" comprises the greater part of ordinary religious life, which the *Tannisho* calls "heretical" and which I refer to as tribalism or half-belief. It is founded on the belief that we can become the instruments of our own spiritual salvation based on what we do—that we can control it, or that we need to. It is based on the belief that the universe is not a good place to be.

To answer Jesus' invitation to follow the Way, it is not sufficient to practice our religion as an act of goodness. Strictly speaking, good acts are impossible, if by that expression we mean acts that make us worthy of being saved. We perform good acts for the sake of themselves, or out of love for God or one another, but not to speed us on our way to the kingdom of heaven. Water on its way to the ocean cannot do anything to become more waterlike. And it can't go slower or faster than it goes. The oneness and majesty of the ocean are beyond its conception and its power. And yet the world itself is constructed in such a manner that water always finds its way.

But how hard it is to relax and simply trust in that. What the self desires more than anything else is the guarantee of its own deliverance. Sadly, it is left to its own devices in imagining what that might entail, so the principal work of selfhood becomes making comparisons. Apart from opposites like good and evil, it has no frame of reference. For its own salvation to exist, it imagines that salvation must have an opposite. The opposite of heaven is hell, the opposite of salvation damnation, so the self begins to imagine a scenario whereby it becomes the *special* object of salvation. In other words, it begins to formulate a salvation of its own, which means another must be damned.

This is the point of the Bible's account of the fall of man. Adam and

Eve are already saved in the garden. They live in harmony with all that is and are daily in the presence of God. Only when the serpent appears, that symbol of incipient selfhood that the Bible describes as "more subtle than any beast of the field which the Lord God had made" (Genesis 3:1), does it begin to seem to them that something is lacking from their experience. They eat from the tree of the knowledge of good and evil in order to "be as gods" (wise and, presumably, capable of effecting their own special salvation), and for the first time experience themselves as lost and alone.

There are no special objects of salvation. This is the essence of the Buddha way, the Christ way, the way of Allah, and—speaking in the broadest possible terms—the way of Life. All are saved. This belief may seem heretical to mainstream Jews, Christians, or Muslims (even to some mainstream Buddhists), but that is only because mainstream religion is itself a form of heresy. Having lost the spirit of revolution, it has long since become a way of preserving our ideas about the self.

Jesus never tired of pointing out this kind of heresy. Once he told the parable of a landowner who went out early in the morning to hire laborers for his vineyard. He offered a day's wages to those he first hired, and then also to those he hired at the third, sixth, ninth, and even the eleventh hour. All were paid a day's wage, whether they worked for twelve hours or only one. Predictably, those who had labored all day protested that they had not received more than the ones who had worked for only an hour—in other words, they complained that they had not come out on top. But the landowner only replied, "Is thine eye evil, because I am good?" (Matthew 20:15).

Indeed, the eyes of human beings *are* evil in comparison to those of God, who causes the rain to fall on both the wicked and the just, and Buddha, who "grasps, never to abandon" all beings with his compassionate light. What could be more fair than to pay a day's wages for any part of a day's work? Such statements challenge the logic of the calculating mind, true enough, but they recognize the deeper logic by which all beings share equally in the Pure Land or the kingdom of heaven, regardless of whatever condition they happen to occupy in this life. What could be more fair than the salvation of all beings, regardless of whether or not they are born in conditions favoring a religiously observant style of life? And yet look how we struggle against that universal law. The person who studies in a learned spiritual tradition like Orthodox Judaism privately believes that one must be learned in order to be saved. The woman who has taken Jesus Christ as her personal savior maintains the literal truth of his claim "I am the way, the truth, and the life: no man cometh unto the Father, but by me" (John 14:6). Theravada Buddhists believe you have to follow the 250 rules of the traditional monastic order to become enlightened.

It is sad to think how much suffering we inflict on ourselves and one another because of this delusion. In the end, we always end up in our own or one another's hell. But even in that there is no cause for fear or alarm. "For everyone who exalts himself will be humbled," says Jesus, "and he who humbles himself will be exalted." Once we accept that and believe it, we experience the true meaning of grace and forgiveness. Top or bottom, good or evil—there is no place we can go where we and all beings together are not already in the kingdom of God.

Naturally, that means I must make my peace even with a Muslim terrorist, and he must make his peace with me. Not to do so is to choose each other's hell—and that is not the kind of destiny that can ever be averted with violence. We find the kingdom of God by seeking it together, or we never find it. Apart from that seeking and that togetherness, there is no kingdom to be found.

23

Lost and Found

What man of you, having an hundred sheep, if he lose one of
them, doth not leave the ninety and nine in the wilderness, and
go after that which is lost, until he find it?

—LUKE 15:4

When the Pharisees criticize Jesus for associating with sinners, he responds with a parable that makes it clear what kind of person comes closest to the experience of divine mercy. It is the lost sheep, the one who wanders off from the fold. What the parable doesn't say outright (because it is the nature of a parable to test with its mysteries the depth of our spiritual resolve) is that the "lost sheep" is precisely the kind of person God can find. The others are too busy finding themselves or one another to allow themselves to be found by God.

When we consider Jesus' parable carefully, it becomes clear that "the ninety and the nine" who are left in the wilderness by the shepherd are just as lost as the one who has wandered off, even though they have no knowledge of this. Their experience of "safety in numbers" gives the illusion of having been found, and so they stop crying out for help. But, in truth, the presence of others has done nothing to mitigate the fact that they have no idea where they really are. They look to one another to answer their existential questions—about who they are and who they are not, what it means to live a good life, and the nature of right and wrong. But the answers they receive from one another are born of consensus, not of God, and so they aren't really answers—at least not *ultimate* answers. They are as lost now as the moment they were born.

Each religious tradition provides a moral context that quite literally frames life and gives it meaning against the inconceivably vast backdrop of astronomical space and time. Practically speaking, that is its purpose. Witness the two driving forces in American evangelical thought today—creationism and millennialism, attempts to fix a beginning and an end-point to time. So strong is the impulse to put a meaningful frame on human existence, to locate it in relationship to all that is, that some Christian authors have published creationist accounts of the age of dinosaurs and the formation of the Grand Canyon. Secularists may criticize them for what seem to be acts of intellectual suicide, but they are none the wiser so long as they refuse to recognize the same impulse in themselves—the overpowering desire to create a frame of reference that gives them the confidence to live and act meaningfully in the world. If the Christian fundamentalist doesn't want to feel lost in the cosmos, the geologist or evolutionary biologist doesn't want to either. *No one* wants to feel lost—even though they are. But the only one who can find us is God himself. God tells us where we are, not the Bible, not the church, not science, and certainly not another person. Only God knows for sure.

Every human being is born into the world knowing nothing. As we grow older, everything we learn is taught to us by other human beings who, like ourselves, were born into the world knowing nothing. If we follow this line of transmission back far enough, we will always come up empty-handed. The only thing that halts the backward slide into eternity is a Jesus or a Buddha or a Muhammad—and that only because they are able to address us at the deepest level of our being, providing a place of purchase and of rest. And even then, only if we believe.

A story recounted in Stephen Hawking's *A Brief History of Time* tells us that once the philosopher Bertrand Russell was concluding a public lecture on astronomy when an old woman stood up at the back of the hall and said, "Mr. Russell, what you've told us is absolute rubbish. The world is really a flat plate resting on the back of a giant turtle."

When the laughter had died down, Russell asked with a knowing smile, "And what, pray tell, Madam, is the turtle standing on?"

But the old woman was a match for him. "You're a very clever young man, no doubt," she answered. "But it's no use—it's turtles all the way down!"

I tend not to believe that the old woman in question was a true believer in some tortoise-based cosmology. Rather, she must have been having some fun at Russell's expense. Listening to his lecture on how the moon orbits the earth, the earth orbits the sun, and even the sun orbits the center of the galaxy, she must have felt a twinge of impatience with such a purely scientific approach to ultimate questions. A part of her must have insisted, "It's all rubbish. Just one fact on top of another, on top of another—all relativistic answers for a mystery that is ultimately beyond all comprehension." Russell's lecture wasn't enough to anchor her in the universe, wasn't emotionally powerful enough to approach anything like belief. And so she thought of a well-known myth that has the earth resting upon the back of a giant tortoise, and laid her trap for the unwitting philosopher, who had her pegged for an ignoramus, when in fact she was only honest. His explanations, as carefully organized, expertly rendered, and empirically verifiable as they were, didn't address the kinds of ultimate questions that all of us without exception carry buried in our hearts—questions that Paul Gauguin wrote in the margin of his most famous painting: "Where do we come from? What are we? Where are we going?"

God finds lost souls. It cannot be put more plainly than that. He will find a lost fundamentalist as easily as a lost neuroscientist. But first they have to become lost—irretrievably and hopelessly lost. And this is not so easy for human beings.

What does it mean to be lost? To be lost is to have exhausted all of our self-motivated agendas and strategies for saving ourselves and thus to have become fully available to God. That is why the Israelites must wander for forty years in the desert before God can lead them to the Promised Land. The distance itself is no more than a few weeks' journey, but to get there they must reach the point where they can allow themselves to be led by God.

One Saturday morning some years ago, I got up early to go shopping at the Woodstock Library Sale. Spiritually speaking, if you are on a budget and looking to find yourself, you can't pick a much better place to start. The storage shed behind the main library building contained, floor to ceiling, several thousand feet of shelf space, not to mention all the tables stacked with box upon box of books on every imaginable subject. Whatever anyone might think about Woodstock as the countercultural nexus of the 1960s, for better or worse, we are a town of readers. Now, as then, the public library is the spiritual and intellectual center of the town.

Ostensibly, that morning I was looking to add to my collection of spiritual books, but really I was hoping to find myself, and still looking for the book that would somehow tell me where I was. But I got sidetracked and wasn't able to get to the library until noon. By then, on a summer Saturday, the spiritual books had been pretty well picked over. Only the usual suspects remained—a well-foxed copy of James Allen's

As a Man Thinketh, circa 1933; a paperback version of *The Practice of the Presence of God;* a dozen or so New Age books of little interest; and twelve Bibles of varied provenance, from Gideon to family heirloom. It was inside this last, an oversized leather edition, that I found a real treasure.

At first it appeared to be a very slim pamphlet, about three inches by six inches in size. But as I removed it from the inside cover of the Bible, I realized that it was actually a book—albeit a very short one—hand stitched and printed on thick, high-quality paper, and obviously crafted with great loving care. It was called *The Journey,* and its text consisted of a single page.

> *Three travelers, having neither map nor goal, became lost along the way.*
> *Said the first, But I was following a star . . .*
> *Said the second, But I was following a road . . .*
> *Said the third, But I was following you. I thought you knew . . . I thought you knew . . .*

There was a single star embossed on the cover and again on the title page, and at the back the inscription "Little Press, Bayport, Christmas 1962," so I assume the speakers in the story must have been the Three Wise Men of the Bible, although from the story itself, there's no way to tell for sure. For years I searched for the couple who had made it—in Bayport, Maine, Bayport, Long Island, and every other Bayport I could think of—but I never found them. And so the book remains a mystery. Likely as not, it was intended as a kind of Christmas card, the authors of which are, at this point, possibly no longer alive.

I paid for the book (actually, the library ladies gave it to me for free because they didn't have change for a quarter) and thereafter I used it as a bookmark in my Bible for nearly seven years. Then one day I looked and it simply wasn't there. By then, however, it had long since become my guide to reading the Bible. But not the kind of guide who reassures you, "Yes, I've passed this way before—the truth is just the other side of that mountain up yonder." This guide said over and over, "Don't look at me. I have no idea where we are. But God will find a way."

We are lost the moment we open the Bible. With its very first words, the Bible seems to cry, "Man overboard!" God, in his infinite mercy, says "Let there be land," and soon we have a dry place to stand. But we still don't know where we are. Even once the Bible gets under way and we seem to have found our footing, once we have been given laws and codes of behavior, and told which land is ours to live on, we are still fundamentally lost. During their years of wandering in the deserts of the Sinai, the Israelites' constant refrain is that they want to go back to Egypt, where, though they were slaves, at least they experienced some certainty. And over and over Moses convinces them to go on.

The spiritual journey cannot be completed by the person who knows the way. Only God knows how to complete that journey. But that doesn't stop us from getting waylaid along the path by one of the many strategies we have for finding ourselves, few of which have anything to do with God.

When the Pharisees accuse him of associating with sinners, Jesus says, "I came not to call the righteous, but sinners to repentance" (Mark 2:17). Another time, he speaks of lost sheep. Today some Christian churches consider it wrong to be a lesbian or a homosexual. These are the sinners they feel ought to repent and come to Jesus, the lost sheep who must be reformed and brought back into the fold. They are within their rights to think so. But do they suppose that they are thereby any less lost? Do they suppose the belief that homosexuality is a sin will somehow save them? According to the teachings of Jesus, just the opposite is true. The outcast, the one who suffers the condemnation of society and is therefore "driven from their midst," is more likely to become lost and helpless. This is just the kind of person God is looking for. Like Jesus, he patrols the borders of communities convinced of their moral rightness, waiting for the very ones they have driven out.

24

Forgiveness

And forgive us our debts, as we forgive our debtors.

—MATTHEW 6:12

When I left the monastery where I had trained, abandoning the monk-hood and returning to the life of a layman, the abbot told the members of the temple where I had been priest that I was going to hell—the *Buddhist* hell. Unlike the Christian version, it wasn't eternal. Eventually you got to leave, transmigrating to one of the other, possibly less painful realms. But it was bad enough. The "Hell of Incessant Suffering" is every bit as bad as its Christian equivalent, replete with burning, torture, and endless deprivation—of light, of love, of anything and everything that is good. And so I think it is safe to say that he meant just what most people do when they say, "Go to hell!" He had no use for me. I had betrayed him, and he was angry—angry enough to cut me out of the Buddha's universal compassion. Angry enough to deny me the grace of God.

To be fair, he had his reasons. I had also cut him out. True, I hadn't told him he was going to hell; my respect for him as a teacher, even then, was such that the thought was a virtual impossibility. But I had rejected his lifestyle, in his mind effectively denying all that I had been taught. And I was leaving him. It was just that simple. We had been as close as father and son—in some ways even closer—and now I was turning my back on all of that.

The night I told him I was leaving, he looked at me with a sadness I'd never seen. It was a completely unguarded moment, the likes of which I had witnessed in him only once or twice before. Usually he was an utterly imposing presence, every inch the Japanese Zen master—calm, centered, and perfectly self-composed, even when he was angry. But in that moment it all fell away. He didn't beg me to stay or to reconsider, although I got the impression he might have had he thought there was any chance I would change my mind. Instead, he said in a voice just a little above a whisper, "How can you say that?"

"I *am* saying it," I answered, because I was certain by that point that I never wanted to be a Zen master, even though I had spent my entire adult life struggling toward that end. His pain and disappointment meant nothing to me at the time—or the fact that he was by then already old enough to retire and would have to start the whole process over again, training someone else to do his job. For all that, he was extremely kind to me over the following months. He only lost it at the end.

A few years later I was married again with children of my own. In retrospect, that was a big part of it. I wanted real children, not just the spiritual children you could have as an abbot. Perhaps that is my failing—I don't know. But it was real. Having children settled me in a way I was never able to get settled on the meditation cushion. Had I known myself better at the time, perhaps I could have saved everyone a lot of misery, including myself.

When I finally returned to visit him after a lapse of many years, I took my family with me. Perdita had been urging me to go back for as long as

I could remember. Not that she wanted me to be a monk again, or even to practice Zen. But she knew me well enough to know how much it weighed on my conscience to have abandoned the man who had been such a father to me. "You don't have to do anything but say hi and introduce him to your family, and you'll feel better," she told me. But that wasn't entirely right.

The visit was underwhelming to say the least. We sat on cushions around the low wooden table in the monastery meeting room, while a young monk (about the age I had been during my monastery days) served us tea and Japanese sweets. Sophie devoured hers with the barely contained enthusiasm of a little girl invited to tea with the queen. Jonah spat his out after one bite and groaned, putting his head on the table, and promptly falling asleep. Through all of this the abbot said almost nothing, making polite, if perfunctory conversation. It felt as if he were entertaining the friends of a very distant relation whom he never expected to see again. Afterward all Perdita could say was "Well, that didn't go exactly as I'd planned." And if that were all there was to it, I'd have to agree. But later that day something happened that changed my view of the entire event and sent me back to see my teacher again the following year.

That afternoon when we returned from the monastery, the phone was ringing as we walked into the house. I dropped our bags inside the door and ran to the kitchen just as the answering machine was picking up. It was my ex-wife, whom I hadn't spoken to in more than fifteen years. She'd called to say that just that morning she'd been going through a closet in her house in Tennessee and found some Zen-style ink paintings I had done years before, and would I like to have them back?

It was all too much. "Yes," I answered finally, when I'd recovered from the shock of hearing her voice again. "That would be great." But then she got to the point. I wasn't sure she'd even known why she called until that moment, but then she just blurted it right out: "Have you forgiven me?"

I hardly knew what to say. True, I'd been mad when we split, but did

I have any right to be angry? I'd abandoned her to become a monk. Worse, I'd married her and lived with her—for nine years altogether, all through our twenties—knowing in my heart that eventually I was going to leave her and become a monk. My life with her had been a betrayal from the start. And I had *loved* her. That was the worst of it. I wasn't sure what I was supposed to forgive. I needed her forgiveness far more than she needed mine. But I gave it anyway, and she gave me hers.

That was what I told my teacher when I went back to see him again the following year, this time alone. He listened to the whole story, after which he said, "Yes, I remember now how sad your wife was when you left her. *So* sad. But now she has forgiven you. And you have forgiven her."

That was all it took. Somehow, then it all just poured out of me. I'd caused *her* so much pain and *him* so much pain, all because I'd been so young and selfish and self-absorbed and hadn't a clue about who I really was. I was sorry for everything and needed his forgiveness. He laughed and said something to the effect that we were *all* much younger then and that mistakes were made. But then later that night, before a group of a hundred or more people, he spoke for nearly an hour about our meeting, albeit without using my name. He talked about the unfathomable ways in which we were all connected to one another, about how what sometimes seemed like a knot of suffering was really a net of interconnected lines that were invisible to the naked eye but nevertheless real—more real even than the world we could see. Change one thing, and everything else shifted. Forgive one person in your life, or seek another's forgiveness, and there was no telling where it would end. I knew him well enough by then to know that this was his way of forgiving me, and asking my forgiveness. It was very Japanese, and very Zen-masterly, but no less complete or sincere.

According to Jesus, the revolutionary message at the heart of the gospel is one thing and one thing only, and that is the forgiveness of sins.

Although the Lord's Prayer contains other petitions—for the hallowing of God's name, the coming of the kingdom, for daily bread, and so forth—when Jesus offered it to his disciples, it was forgiveness he spoke about afterward, to make it clear to them that, practically speaking, this was the true point of the prayer: "For if ye forgive men their trespasses, your heavenly Father will also forgive you: But if ye forgive not men their trespasses, neither will your Father forgive your trespasses" (Matthew 6:14–15). Practice forgiveness and the rest is taken care of, Jesus taught. Practice forgiveness, and the kingdom of God will come.

But we must *participate* in forgiveness in order to experience it. We can't just ask God for grace and be done with it. We get only as good as we give. We must become a channel through which forgiveness can flow. Only then can we be at peace with the cosmos, experiencing it as the fundamentally good place that God intended it to be.

The world, which seems to us to be driven by the forces of monetary economies, the never-ending cycle of daily give-and-take, is in reality driven by an economy of grace whose various indices and portfolios can't be reckoned in the ordinary way. We don't forgive others and then receive forgiveness from God, in payment for services rendered. We receive forgiveness in the *act* of forgiveness. There is no cause and effect in this equation. The effect is simultaneous. There is no lapse of time.

Realistically, however, it may take a long time to learn this. Just because we repeat the words of the prayer, that doesn't mean we understand them, much less that we are able to actually do what they say. The weight of unforgiveness in our lives is so massive it sits before us like a mountain we can't see around. It blocks our view of everything. But as big as it is, and as close as we are to it with our endless grievances against God and ourselves, and one another, and the world, we don't even know it is there. We simply go on living in its shadow, getting by the best we can. Occasionally we get a little sunlight to console or inspire us, but for the most part there seems to be nothing we can do to move it out of the way. "If ye shall say unto this mountain, Be thou removed, and be thou cast into the sea; it shall be done," says Jesus (Matthew 21:21). But first we must know that it is there.

The essence of the Lord's Prayer is that we feel forgiven when we forgive. It is the realization that we can pray for everyone, that we can include everyone in heaven—even our enemies—and that in so doing, we get to be there, too.

25

A New Birth

Nicodemus saith unto him, How can a man be born
when he is old? can he enter the second time
into his mother's womb, and be born?

—JOHN 3:4

Nicodemus, "a ruler of the Jews," once came to see Jesus under cover of
night. A member of the ruling council of Jerusalem, he represented the
established religion of the day, with the moral authority of its laws and
customs at his disposal, and the strength of its political and economic
might. So why did he feel it necessary to visit the renegade rabbi from
Galilee? And in the middle of the night, no less. What kept him up so
late? What made him risk the censure of his peers? Why not just rest secure in the rightness of his religious sensibility? Why not leave well
enough alone?

Apparently, because he couldn't. The teachings of Jesus, spread by
word of mouth in recent days until the great city of Jerusalem was ablaze
with them, had left Nicodemus in a state of profoundest doubt. He had
discovered something about himself that he had always half suspected

but had never had the courage to confess to anyone before. He was a half-believer. Nicodemus, the man looked up to as a religious authority of his day, didn't know what it meant to truly believe in God.

"Rabbi, we know that thou art a teacher come from God," Nicodemus begins, "for no man can do these miracles that thou doest, except God be with him" (John 3:2). It isn't exactly a question. But then it isn't a statement either. Rather, it's a confession in disguise. Because what Nicodemus means is simply this: "I thought I spoke for God, that I was doing his will by following the letter of the law and teaching others to do the same, but when I listen to you, Rabbi, I realize that I don't speak for God and never have. I don't know what my religion is anymore. I don't know what any of it means." Or, at any rate, that is what Jesus *hears*—not the words from Nicodemus's lips, but the meaning from his heart. That is why he answers as he does: "Verily, verily, I say unto thee, Except a man be born again, he cannot see the kingdom of God" (John 3:3).

When Jesus spoke about being born again it was not yet a Christian term. Jesus was a Jew, and it was as a Jew that he spoke to Nicodemus—one Jew to another. To talk about being born again was at that time a radical Jewish idea, and both Jesus and Nicodemus knew what was at stake in contemplating it together. Nicodemus, the high priest, stood for the traditions and laws of institutional Judaism, and all the power, prestige, and possessions that came along with his priestly status. He represented what people already had, what they already knew, and what they already believed, and his responsibility was to protect all of that. Jesus, on the other hand, embodied the prophetic impulse in Judaism. The purpose of his ministry was not to support the externals of the law, but to find the spirit of that law, to liberate it, and to allow it to reenter the lives of ordinary people through the experience he called being "born again."

Born again . . .

The New Revised Standard Version translates the words as "born from above," making it clear that that experience comes to us *vertically,* directly from God, rather than *laterally,* through the mediation of institutionalized religious practice or doctrinal belief.

Early Christians (most of whom were Jewish) experienced being born again as a birthing out of their existing individual and cultural story line, and into a much more fluid state of being where religious observance was largely improvisational and their status as Christians set them against the prevailing norm. Indeed, they could be killed for it. Thus, to a would-be disciple who tells Jesus he will follow him anywhere, Jesus warns, "Foxes have holes, and birds of the air have nests; but the Son of man hath not where to lay his head" (Luke 9:58).

In fact, Jesus presents a very different view of conversion than we find in most religious circles today, where we tend to be born *into* our existing religious contexts rather than *out* of them, and where the converted are therefore more likely to find the safety in numbers and the political clout that come from being shareholders in whatever monolithic religious denomination they happen to belong to. About the real meaning of conversion, Jesus is unequivocal. In the face of that exclusionist mentality encouraged by religious institutions, then and now, he calls for a radical reorganization of our loyalties to the world, in which traditional tribal affiliations are superseded by a much broader and deeper set of spiritual responsibilities and social concerns. Thus he says, "If any man come to me, and hate not his father, and mother, and wife, and children, and brethren, and sisters, yea, and his own life also, he cannot be my disciple" (Luke 14:26).

Can Jesus have meant to invalidate the commandment to honor one's father and mother? Not if we understand his real intent. His problem is not with the family itself or with the larger, somewhat less cohesive social group we call a town or country, but with the small-minded parochialism that results when tribal loyalties are seen as an end in themselves, displacing principles of fairness, common decency, and simple brotherly love.

Once Jesus' mother and his brothers came to see him in a town where he was teaching by the sea. The content of his social gospel, as radical by first-century standards as it is today, had already begun to draw the attention of the authorities. Presumably, they were worried for his safety and wanted to bring him home. But when told by the multitude that his mother and brothers were waiting to see him, Jesus only looked around at the crowd and said, "Behold my mother and my brethren!" (Mark 3:34)

And so, while Jesus' words run counter to the nostalgic, quasi-patriotic return to the customs and cultural norms of yesteryear that today are sometimes called "family values," he nevertheless champions the true meaning of family, extending its message of love and protection to all others throughout the world. Even the language he uses reflects this truth. His God is a loving father, and all men are his brothers.

This is the new birth Jesus speaks of, in which we find ourselves united from above by a single Father, a universal source of love that spreads above us like the desert sky. Like the sky, that experience happens everywhere without exception. And like the sky, it can happen to anyone—conservative, liberal, charismatic, evangelical, secular humanist, or fundamentalist. No one owns the sky. It can happen to a Hindu . . . and he doesn't have to stop being a Hindu. It can happen to a Jew . . . and she doesn't have to stop being a Jew.

In actual practice, however, the universality of that born-again experience is often lost sometime after the fact. It seems there is an inevitable human impulse to put that experience inside a box, to try to preserve or protect it, to contain it inside a set of ideas or principles we can control and understand. But that impulse always has the effect of reducing its scope and power in the end, bringing it down to the scale of ordinary tribal life. And so we have to ask ourselves a simple question: what kind of world are we born to when we are born again? Are we merely reborn into the narrow shoe box of our own culturally conditioned prejudices and beliefs? Or are we born *out* of all that, and *to* a truly different kind of reality? Is being born again a one-time affair, an experience that negates all that came before it and sanctions all that follows, or is it something that happens to us over and over again, a constant renewal of life through the gospel of universal forgiveness and love?

Have you ever held your breath to see how long you can keep it inside of your lungs? What's the longest? A minute? Maybe two? It quickly becomes empty air. And yet, this presents no problem for us. As soon as we let go of the breath we are holding, we get another . . . and another. So we never bother to hold our breath. Breathing is the "knowledge," entirely visceral, that we don't have to hold on to the breath because, even though it comes and goes with every moment, it is always there. In the same way, being born from above brings with it the "knowledge" that we don't have to know anything. "For it shall be given you in that same hour what ye shall speak," Jesus tells his disciples (Matthew 10:19). The breath of spirit is forever arriving and departing—but it is always, *always* there. We are not a receptacle for that spirit—we are not its container, its protector, or its master. We embrace that spirit as an open channel, or we don't embrace it at all. Capture the wind and it isn't wind anymore. Put it inside a box, and immediately it becomes nothing but empty air.

In order to be born again in the open-ended, ongoing way that Jesus advocates, we must begin by recognizing ourselves as Nicodemus. Like him, we come to the spiritual life with our god-in-a-box—which is to say, with a very little, very small-minded god we can carry with us wherever we go and whose will we can therefore control. Occasionally we let him out of that box—when disaster strikes, or joy, or unexpected love—but for the most part we are content to have him where he is. Nevertheless, like Nicodemus, we sense that something is amiss. Then, one day, from somewhere news reaches us of another God, a God that spreads above us like the sky, a God whose spirit rushes in like the wind, sweeping away the collective dust of calcified religion, giving us the feeling of being born anew. When we hear news of that God, we naturally want to seek him out. And yet, we have no choice but to go as we are, with the little, small-minded god of our own imagination carried securely under one arm. That is how we are made, and it is infinitely forgivable, so long as we are willing to surrender that small god to the One God once the wind of spirit begins to blow.

That, I believe, is what happens to Nicodemus. "How can a man be born when he is old?" he asks, and Jesus answers: "The wind blows where it wishes, and you hear the sound of it, but cannot tell where it comes from and where it goes. So is everyone who is born of the Spirit" (John 3:8).* In other words, it is an experience that comes to us from beyond ourselves. When that happens, we will know it with a knowledge as natural as breathing in and out. Because once the box is open, the kingdom of heaven has no choice but to appear.

---

*New King James Version.

26

The Moral Center

So when they continued asking him, he lifted up himself,

and said unto them, He that is without sin among you,

let him first cast a stone at her.

—JOHN 8:7

In the gospel of John, Jesus is asked to decide the fate of an unfaithful woman. It is early in the morning, and the scribes and Pharisees have driven her to the steps of the temple where Jesus is teaching. "Master, this woman was taken in adultery, in the very act," they proclaim. "Now Moses in the law commanded us, that such should be stoned: but what sayest thou?" (John 8:4–5).

It is a clever trap. If Jesus tells them to let her go free, he violates the letter of Jewish law. If he says to stone her, he betrays its spirit. Faced with an impossible choice, Jesus wisely says nothing. Instead, he stoops and begins writing on the ground with his finger.

The woman's accusers ask him yet again, "But what sayest thou?" "So when they continued asking him, he lifted himself, and said unto them, He that is without sin among you, let him first cast a stone at her.

And again he stooped down, and wrote on the ground" (John 8:9). The rest we know. "And they which heard it, being convicted by their own conscience, went out one by one, beginning at the eldest, even unto the last: and Jesus was left alone, and the woman standing in the midst" (John 8:9).

A remarkable story in every sense. The hapless woman. The teacher. The insidious trap. And at the last possible moment the "turning word" with which she is liberated and those who have accused her are made to see firsthand that what the Bible calls "the law" cannot be read from the periphery of their being—from the point of view of their petty, socially conditioned phobias, preferences, and prejudices—but only from the moral center of their lives.

What is the moral center that Jesus finds when he stoops to write with his finger in the dust, so that when he stands again to confront the woman's accusers he speaks with the voice of moral authority? And what, if anything, does it have to do with the writing on the ground?

The traditional commentaries offer various explanations for this, the only instance in the Bible when Jesus was said to write anything. Some claim that he was writing the commandments. Others, the names of the woman's accusers. And still others that, next to those names, he is writing down their sins. But really, it could be anything. The Bible doesn't say. It isn't *what* Jesus writes that matters, but that it was *written on the ground.*

The earth is what we come from, the place where we live and breathe while we are alive, and what we return to when we die. Thus, every human life is a story written on the ground. "For dust thou art," God tells Adam, "and unto dust shalt thou return" (Genesis 3:19). We would like to think better of ourselves, but this is the simple truth of it. We are dust. Only when we forget this do we lose our center, and along with it the compassion for others that is the basis for all truly moral acts. But, of course, this happens all the time. To act from our moral center is for most of us the exception, not the rule.

The Pure Land teacher Shuichi Maida once wrote that "the evil person"—the one who is in touch with his mortality and thus also with the moral center—cannot even claim the right to exist. "The evil person might as well be annihilated. He is just like a leaf being blown away by the dry winds of autumn." And yet it is that very "leaf nature," he insisted, that allows us to smile despite the uncertainty of existence. The person who cannot claim a right to exist has no choice but to smile, Maida wrote. Only a smile expresses the freedom we feel by entrusting ourselves, leaf in wind, to a Power Beyond the Self.

Jesus himself never departs from this awareness, and thus the moral center is never farther than the dust beneath his feet. He bends to touch it and immediately knows what to say. "He that is without sin among you, let him first cast a stone at her." He understood that we can withhold forgiveness from another only when we have forgotten that forgiveness is the thing we most have need of ourselves. To remember this is to find our own moral center. To forget it is to run afoul of all that is worst in human nature.

At the end of World War II, when the Allied forces created a tribunal to prosecute crimes against humanity, a German-speaking army psychiatrist named Gustave Gilbert was assigned the duty of evaluating the mental health of defendants, monitoring them for suicidal behavior throughout the duration of the trial. To that end, Gilbert was granted unrestricted access to the elite Nazi leadership who had been responsible for the worst atrocities of the Holocaust. Contemplating the question that was then foremost in everybody's mind—namely, how such seemingly intelligent, cultured people could have committed acts of unimaginable cruelty against other human beings—he finally concluded that it was due to lack of empathy. That was the one personality characteristic that all the defendants had in common: a genuine inability to put themselves in the place of their fellow man. "Evil, I think, is the absence of empathy," said Gilbert.

The awareness that we are sustained by a Power Beyond the Self, that we do not cause ourselves to be and cannot preserve our lives alone, absent the blessings bestowed upon us in every moment of every day—by those who grow the food we eat, by those who protect us from grief or harm, by the very air we breathe—this awareness itself is the basis for empathy. Other Power is the moral foundation for our lives. To talk about good and evil apart from a Power Beyond the Self is to invite the most profound moral lapses human beings are capable of—from the Holocaust to global warming. We cannot risk speaking of good and evil unless we first speak of God.

During the rise of German fascism (and its equivalent in Japan), a Pure Land priest named Ishin Yoshimoto was developing a form of psychotherapy called Naikan, or self-reflection. A businessman by training, Yoshimoto was used to looking at human behavior in terms of commerce: the exchange of money for goods and services that forms the basis of any economy. Yoshimoto came to believe that gratitude—the awareness that we receive from the world and others far more than we can ever repay—was the fundamental basis for all human morality and therefore the real secret of happiness. And gratitude came from a clear understanding of the working Other Power in our lives.

To cultivate that awareness, Yoshimoto devised a treatment based on three simple questions:

1. What have I received?
2. What have I given?
3. What troubles and difficulties have I caused?

He believed we should ask those three questions, starting at the center, by addressing them to the first significant persons in our life: our mother and father. From there we could apply them to a host of "significant others"—a sibling or a spouse, a friend, a teacher, or a neighbor. Eventually we could apply them to everything and everyone in our lives. Ultimately, we could apply those same three questions to the earth itself. What have we received from the earth? What have we given? What problems have we caused? Some Western psychologists have voiced concern about Yoshimoto's methods, suggesting that they might foster a morbid sense of guilt. Had they taken them to their natural conclusion, however, they would have discovered the joy of surrender that comes of realizing that our lives lie dead center of a field of blessing that we could never ever repay, much less deserve. True enough, that experience creates humility, but that humility also gives rise to joy. And that joy—born of a lack of self-importance—becomes the basis for all moral action in the world.

Once we have that joy, we cannot imagine taking it from another, or taking away the potential for it in those who are currently oppressed, downtrodden, or alone. Finally, that is the most remarkable thing about the story of Jesus and the woman taken in adultery. We are told that those who heard his words, "being convicted by their own conscience, went out one by one." But we aren't told what happened to them afterward. Perhaps they joined their own first-century version of a fascist mob. Or perhaps not. Isn't it possible that some, at least, took his words profoundly to heart?

Give what we may, we cannot repay the price for even one second of life. This knowledge is the basis for gratitude, and thus the moral dimension of life. Self-righteous morality, which is to say, morality apart from gratitude, is by contrast a kind of living hell. There is no mercy in that hell, only retribution. Thus we may sometimes feel tempted to say, "I deserve to suffer less in my life, while my neighbor deserves to suffer more," but few of us are willing to confront the far deeper, more obvious truth that none of us have done anything, anything at all, to deserve the incomparable gift of that life. And yet we are given it in full.

27

The Needle's Eye

It is easier for a camel to go through the eye of a needle,
than for a rich man to enter into the kingdom of God.

—MARK 10:25

One day not long after I became a priest at the Zen temple in Manhattan, I received a call from my teacher, the abbot, telling me to quickly don my robes and meet him at an address in midtown Manhattan. "Hurry," he added before hanging up the phone, "and bring the special incense."

I disliked wearing my monk's robes out on the street, but I did as instructed and was deposited by taxi a few minutes later in front of an upscale apartment building where the abbot joined me in the lobby. "What is this about?" I asked as we rode the elevator up together, but he answered only that a great friend of the temple had died. In that case I couldn't see what the hurry was, but I kept that thought to myself. A moment later we were ushered into a lavish apartment by a middle-aged woman, and from there into a room whose walls were covered floor to ceiling with the most extraordinary elaborate needlework tapestries and sunburst quilts that I had ever seen. And there, in the midst of them all, lying in bed, was the body of the woman who, as I learned later, had made them.

Her head lay tilted back as though she'd been gazing at something just above and slightly behind her, her long gray hair lying braided on the pillow, her mouth open and rounded in the shape of a perfect bowl. And I understood at once why we had hurried. It wasn't for this woman. It had been for me. The abbot, who could have come alone, had brought me to witness what Buddhists called "birth in the Pure Land." Five minutes later and it would have been over. Whatever Jesus said about it being difficult for those with riches to enter the kingdom of God, this was surely an exception. And I stood for a long time, barely mindful of the words of the Buddhist sutra that slipped from my lips as I chanted with my teacher, while smoke trickled upward from the long sticks of incense we held upright in our hands. Suddenly the needle's eye didn't seem so small as I'd always thought. This woman's soul had just passed through it. Her body was a bow still quivering from which the arrow had flown.

At the time I knew nothing about Milly Johnstone but this. Afterward, we made arrangements for a service at the temple and then departed. For a while I was speechless. Finally I asked the obvious question, "Who *was* that woman?" and the abbot replied that she was a very special student of the Buddha dharma. The fact that she and her husband had raised much of the money to pay for the temple was, while important in itself, just the tip of it. Hopefully I would get to know her in the coming months, he mused.

I had no idea what he was talking about, but a week later I found myself on the phone talking with various people who had known her as a friend or teacher or student, and gradually I began to get a sense of her life. One man, a master of a famous Japanese tea school in New York, told a remarkable story.

Milly discovered the tea ceremony during the sixties, when Zen Buddhism was becoming popular in the West, and devoted many years to mastering the elaborate rituals of its arcane discipline. In Japan, *Cha-do*, the Way of Tea, has been passed down for generations as a secular form of spirituality traditionally favored by the religious and political elite.

Once when Milly was performing the tea ceremony for a group of delegates from the United Nations, she committed a seemingly unforgivable lapse of etiquette. No sooner had the guests been seated on the tatami mats than Milly rose from her position before the low iron kettle and excused herself from the room with no explanation. In fact, she excused herself from the apartment altogether, leaving her guests alone. The moment before, some construction workers in the next building had begun demolition on the floor just opposite the tea room, raising an enormous racket. A lesser tea master would probably have drawn the blinds and proceeded to perform the ceremony anyway, leaving his guests to marvel at his poise and concentration under duress. But not Milly.

A few minutes later, she reentered the tea room followed by a half dozen extremely dusty-looking men, each carrying his hard hat respectfully under one arm. They seated themselves on the floor next to the UN delegates, and they all took tea together. The construction workers, unaware of the exacting nature of the ritual they had been invited to, were nevertheless charmed by the American woman in full kimono who insisted, politely but firmly, that they join the ceremony rather than disrupt it. But the Japanese delegates must have realized that, in one simple stroke, Milly Johnstone had cut through four centuries of tradition, to lay bare the heart of a ceremony most people had long since forgotten the meaning of: to embrace all things and all people in a single cup of tea.

But of course this doesn't happen on its own, and that is why Jesus said that it is hard for a rich person—the person full of self-importance, regardless of wealth—to enter the kingdom of God. In Milly's case, the call to that kingdom came in a bizarre and tragic way. One day at the estate where she was living with her first husband, a wolf escaped from the private zoo they owned and killed her four-year-old son. The event shattered her in a way only a truly inexplicable tragedy can, and thereafter she had no choice but to embark on a journey. In Milly's case the journey was a well-financed one, and she was able to visit other countries and meet many accomplished masters. But it was no less arduous or painful to complete, riches affecting only the form that journey takes and not its substance. Finally she found Zen Buddhism and the tea ceremony, and there she found her home. There, and in the extraordinary needlepoint tapestries for which she is famous.

The image of a wolf appears often in Milly's tapestries. All along the lower border of one (*The Peaceable Kingdom*, 1960) she stitched the words of Isaiah 11:6: "The wolf also shall dwell with the lamb and the leopard shall lie down with the kid. And the calf and the young lion together and a little child shall lead them." It is an extraordinary work. At the center of the upper portion, the board of directors of Bethlehem Steel Corporation, where her husband, William Johnstone, was vice president, is celebrating the Last Supper in the style of da Vinci. Surrounding the boardroom on either side and above is the mill itself, with its foundry works, its dark girders, and its fire-belching smokestacks. Below is the world created by God, filled to the brim with lions and bears, trees and vines, rabbits, chickens, geese, and—slightly left of center, just opposite the heart of a person standing directly before the tapestry—a great gray wolf lying peacefully on its side with its forepaw embracing a little lamb. It is an extraordinarily radical vision of inclusion that, according to fiber-arts specialist Barbara Schulman, led Milly to rip out and redo the stitching for the chairman of the board three times in an effort "to make him look less frightened." In a world where all things are included under the loving gaze of God, nothing—and no one—can possibly be left out.

A famous story from the gospels tells us that once when Jesus was passing by on the street, a rich young man came running after him to ask how he could be assured of entry into the kingdom of God. Follow the commandments set down in the Torah, Jesus told him, but the young man insisted that he had observed these all his life:

> Then Jesus beholding him loved him, and said unto him, One thing thou lackest: go thy way, sell whatsoever thou hast, and give to the poor, and thou shalt have treasure in heaven: and come, take up the cross, and follow me. And he was sad at that saying, and went away grieved: for he had great possessions.
>
> (MARK 10:21–22)

That is the moment when Jesus famously observed to his disciples that it was easier for a camel to pass through the eye of a needle than for a rich man to enter the kingdom of God.

And yet, finally, the story had nothing to do with riches—not in the literal sense at least. We know this because of the reaction of Jesus' disciples, who, being as poor as he was, presumably would have had no trouble passing through. But the Gospel of Mark tells us that, upon hearing Jesus' words, "they were astonished out of measure, saying among themselves, Who then can be saved?" (Mark 10:26).

It is easy to love the disciples at this moment. So often they are bickering, faithless, uncharitable, and unwise, and so even while we may identify with them, they are sometimes difficult to hold in affection. But not here. How easy it would have been for them to think that because they were followers of Jesus they were assured a place in the kingdom. But they do not. Hearing Jesus' pronouncement, they are struck to the quick. In their own eyes they are camels, as surely as the rich young man. There is something each and every one of them will not or cannot give up. And that something is the self. We are *all* camels. Saints and sinners, buddhas and bumblers alike, and regardless of our level of material well-being, we are all too big to make it through a needle's eye. We are too full of attachments and aversions—too full of *ourselves*—to enter freely into the boundless wisdom and compassion of the mind of God.

That is the point of the story. The self doesn't reach as far as that kingdom. There is no way we can enter it on our own. That is why Jesus tells the disciples: "With men it is impossible, but not with God: for with God all things are possible" (Mark 10:27).

And that is the sticking point. We can mortify the flesh through fasting, hone our minds with meditation, and reduce our self-importance to the size of a thread by submitting to every law of the Torah, the New Testament, or the Qur'an, and *still* we can never pass through the needle's eye so long as our object is to pass through it alone. That is the point of Jesus' words to the rich young ruler and the point of Milly's tea ceremony and of her needlework portrayal of the peaceable kingdom. We can feel ourselves included in the kingdom of God only when we ourselves exclude nothing from its scope. It is a simple truth, but an uncompromising one: *that which we cannot call good is the subject of all our spiritual work.*

In the end it all comes down to the same point, stated over and over again throughout the Bible in the hope that we will eventually get it. We are to love God by loving one another, including all creation. And where the experience of that love is concerned, we get as good as we give. For those with riches, it may be money they have to give, but money itself is not the point. Money without love can never reach as far as the kingdom. Love alone takes us there. The kingdom itself is love.

28

The Sign of the Kiss

But Jesus said unto him, Judas, betrayest thou

the Son of man with a kiss?

—LUKE 22:48

Jesus is always betrayed by those who profess to love him, by the very ones who claim to be his disciples or his friends. This means that the real enemy of Christianity, today as in Jesus' time, is not the nonbeliever, the infidel, or some other externalized foe. The real enemy of Jesus lies within the fold.

On the night before his crucifixion, Judas appears in the Garden of Gethsemane with those who have come to arrest Jesus. Earlier he has given them a sign: "Whomsoever I shall kiss, that same is he: hold him fast" (Matt. 26:48). Jesus has warned the disciples frequently that his moment will come. Earlier, overcome by a moment of intense religious conviction, they tell him they are certain that he is the Christ, the son of the living God. But he only replies humbly, and with profound sadness, "Have not I chosen you twelve, and one of you is a devil?" (John 6:70). The danger always comes from within.

If all men are our brothers and even our enemies ought to be loved and prayed for, then it is clear that in Christianity there can be no external foe. Even the more apocalyptic passages of the Bible that speak of an Antichrist or devil, if given the intimate reading they require, are a finger pointing toward the self. We live in a time when the enemies of Jesus may very well turn out to be those among us who bear the sign of this kiss— those who would most loudly and publicly profess their belief.

In the unwavering confidence of its own moral vision, mainstream Christianity has lost the knack for self-reflection. Like the person living in a house without mirrors, it can no longer see what it looks like to the world outside its walls. Nor can it imagine how Jesus himself might see it were he to return to earth in the very Second Coming that so many Christians eagerly await.

In first-century Palestine, likewise, there were those who expected the arrival of a messiah, a leader who would become king of Israel, leading a popular revolt against its Roman oppressors. Indeed, when Jesus was crucified, the inscription above his head read "King of the Jews," in mockery of this political dream. But Jesus himself said, "My kingdom is not of this world" (John 18:36). If his kingdom were of this world, he tells us, his disciples would fight and he would not have to die upon a cross. In fact, Jesus' disciples could quite easily have become the terrorists of their day, leading a popular revolt against the Romans, but they did not. Jesus was not that kind of revolutionary.

It is hard to figure how a religion founded upon the ministry of a man who, rather than betray his gospel of forgiveness, became the willing victim of an unjust execution could itself become so militant and warlike. Hard to understand how it could have such a dismal history of intolerance and oppression. The recent alignment of conservative Christianity with the so-called patriotic war on terror is but the latest in a long list of betrayals of Jesus' original moral vision that began on the day when the Emperor Constantine first marched into battle with the cross of Jesus on his shield. Church and state will make cozy bedfellows if we let them, but they will always lead to war.

Jesus' views on the separation of church and state are unambiguously clear: "Render therefore unto Caesar the things which are Caesar's; and unto God the things that are God's" (Matthew 22:21). Our founding fathers, understanding how easily religious intolerance could poison the life of the body politic, established a doctrine of religious freedom for the New World that has served it well for more than two hundred years. What is sometimes overlooked is the fact that, for the founding fathers, the separation of church and state was the positive expression of their Christian moral vision, rather than an attempt to limit its influence on American life. In 1790, a year before the Bill of Rights was ratified, in a letter to Moses Seixas, the warden of Touro Synagogue in Newport, Rhode Island, George Washington wrote of the United States as a land "which gives to bigotry no sanction, to persecution no assistance" and, quoting the prophet Micah, assured him that here "every one shall sit in safety under his own vine and fig tree, and there shall be none to make him afraid" (Micah 4:4).

Even before the Constitution was on the drafting board, some New World Christians were already asserting the independence of their moral vision from traditional tribal loyalties, refusing to allow their religion to be used as a tool of oppression. In the Flushing Remonstrance, a letter drafted in 1657 to Dutch governor Peter Stuyvesant in response to his request that they expel all Quakers from their community, a group of English farmers in what is now Queens, New York, wrote:

The law of love, peace and liberty in the states extending to Jews, Turks and Egyptians, as they are considered sons of Adam, which is the glory of the outward state of Holland, soe love, peace and liberty, extending to all in Christ Jesus, condemns hatred, war and bondage. And because our Saviour sayeth it is impossible but that

offences will come, but woe unto him by whom they cometh, our
desire is not to offend one of his little ones, in whatsoever form,
name or title hee appears in, whether Presbyterian, Independent,
Baptist or Quaker, but shall be glad to see anything of God in any
of them, desiring to doe unto all men as we desire all men should
doe unto us, which is the true law both of Church and State; for
our Saviour sayeth this is the law and the prophets.

Today, Flushing is sometimes said to be the most religiously and ethnically diverse community on earth, with more than one hundred different languages spoken daily on its streets—a kind of Babel in reverse, where those who had been scattered, after their many journeys, have at last come home again. Only this time, nobody talks of building a tower. It is enough for each to have his own vine and fig tree, and for none to make him afraid.

Finally, that is the true goal of religion, and therefore its highest expression. And that itself may be what the prophet Micah had in mind when he spoke of vines and fig trees and of an age of global peace. For hadn't God already given a vine to Jonah to shade him from the heat of the sun? Jonah loved the vine (his own people and his own way of life) but not the Ninevites. And so God sent a worm to destroy the vine. In the same way, every religion ultimately flourishes or fails based solely on its attitude toward others. For no religion can be destroyed from without— the true enemy always lies within. God tries to tell Jonah this, just as the Flushing farmers tried to tell it to Peter Stuyvesant, and George Washington and Thomas Jefferson tried to tell it to their more strident religious neighbors. It is always the impulse to protect or privilege our own religion that undoes it in the end. The other we fear is always our deliverance in disguise.

In the final analysis, I do not believe it is necessary, or even possible, for Christians to be able to understand the world through the eyes of

Muslims, or Muslims through the eyes of Jews. Nor is it necessary for Buddhists to adopt the beliefs of Hindus or Christians, or Christians the practices of Hindus, Buddhists, or Jews. These things will happen or not, and only time and history will tell. We must only love our neighbors as ourselves, as Buddha taught, as Confucius taught, as Moses taught, and as Jesus and Muhammad taught, too. This is not a complicated teaching, and no one owns the rights to it but the one who practices it, and such a person is never selfish about sharing it. That is the only thing that keeps our vine and our fig tree from withering. It provides us with the only true shade and comfort to be had in this world.

For all that, it seems like almost too simple a prescription to be effective. When we think of all the complex ways we interact with one another in the modern world, it is hard to imagine that the solution could be anything as simple as empathy—the willingness to feel what others feel and the readiness to embrace their suffering or happiness as our own. But this is the truth, and as complex and convoluted as our way may become, the journey back to that truth is as simple as asking ourselves a simple question: what is it that we really want out of life?

The answer to that question, while it may take many specific forms, is always some version of fulfillment, safety, or satisfaction—in other words, it is always happiness in the end. In which case what is required of us, if we wish to embrace the life of true belief, is only one small step further. We have only to admit to ourselves that our happiness is tied in the most intimate ways possible to the happiness of others. The universe is made that way. We are saved together or not at all—all forms of selective salvation are illusory.

There is no God who selects us apart from the rest of creation for some special dispensation, leaving out the rest of humanity, and the rest of nature besides. Such a God would not *be* God, but a powerless idol. The modern intellectuals who have challenged the existence of God are surely right to do so if it is this God they challenge. Such a God does not in truth exist. Nor has he any right to. But, finally, the universe itself saves us from such a God. It recognizes the claims of no special class of being but embraces everyone and everything within itself. It even tolerates our illusions. But we cannot find happiness, either in life or religion, so long as we believe in a God who isn't true.

In the end, I think that is the reason why we need to use the teachings of one religion to read the teachings of another, as I have done with Buddhism in this book. It breaks the monopoly we hold on salvation as believers in the teachings of the Bible. The same can be done by using the Bible to read the Buddhist sutras, or the Qur'an to read the Torah. It isn't that we must find meaningful parallels between the various religious traditions of the world, or that we should conform or unify them so that the fundamental integrity of each is lost. We must simply detribalize those teachings so that they can no longer be used as weapons. That must surely be what Micah intended when he wrote: "And they shall beat their swords into plowshares, and their spears into pruninghooks: nation shall not lift up a sword against nation, neither shall they learn war any more" (Isaiah 2:4). Only, in most cases, we persist in thinking literally of weapons when we read such verses, and fail to realize that for the half-believer religion is *always* a weapon. Only belief restores religion to its original purpose—to bring all beings together before God.

29

The Cry on the Cross

And at the ninth hour Jesus cried with a loud voice, saying,

Eloi, Eloi, lama sabachthani? which is, being interpreted,

My God, my God, why hast thou forsaken me?

—MARK 15:34

Often it is the things that happen to us near the beginning of the spiritual journey that turn out to be the most important later on. When we embark on that journey it seems to us that most of our blessings are to come. But God doesn't work that way. He gives us the gifts we need to sustain us on our way right from the beginning, though it may take some years to learn how to use them.

In 1983 I was living on the second floor of a little duplex in the San Marco area of Jacksonville, Florida, not fifty yards from the St. Johns River. Even the names of those places seem loaded with significance now, but at the time I was insensitive to them. My Christian upbringing was a thing I took for granted and mostly tried to live down. I had been studying Zen Buddhism for six or seven years already and, considering the trajectory of my spiritual life, was then at the farthest point in my orbit away

from the religion I'd grown up with. It simply wasn't part of my consciousness. At least, not that I knew.

Then, one night in early March, I had a dream—if you could call it
that. The truth is, I still don't know what to call it. It defied classification.
In fact, for many years I simply didn't know what to do with it. I tried to
interpret it, but could not. I tried to forget it, but that proved impossible, too. Someone from our Thursday night Bible study group once
came up with the image of a fishhook to describe what happens to us
when we get a piece of the Bible stuck inside of us. We would like to
swallow it—to metabolize it, or believe in it, or simply to find some
place for it in our lives—but we cannot. And so we try to spit it back
out, but we can't do that either. So it stays lodged within us, like a fishhook caught in our throats. We can't swallow it, and we can't spit it out.
It remains within us as an irritant until the moment comes when we
find out what it means.

Call it a dream.

I am walking through a forest of tall trees near the end of day. The
weather is overcast, and the last sunlight is seeping through from the
west. There is no path; nevertheless I keep walking straight ahead. My
steps make no sound on the golden pine needles that completely cover
the ground.

As I walk, the voices of men and women come to me from somewhere off to my left. They speak of the future, of every last event that will
occur over the course of my life, up to and including my death. They explain what all of this means in the larger scheme of things. Then, suddenly, I come upon a small clearing, and all this is erased from my mind.
In the clearing stands a great gray stone roughly the shape of an egg half-
buried in the ground. I know that I must embrace it with my whole body,
but I am certain that if I do I will be obliterated. But the only thing I can
recall from what I have been told about my future is that I will embrace

it nevertheless. And so I step forward and, stretching my arms wide, lean my body against the stone.

At that moment I am told that I have been dreaming, but that now I am awake and that what I am about to witness is real and is happening now. And in that instant something extremely peculiar happens to the stone. It doesn't transform exactly. Rather the whole universe shifts around it and suddenly it isn't a stone anymore but an upright wooden beam, and my arms, rather than being spread out as they were before, are now close to my body, my hands holding either side of the beam, my head leaning hard against the wood.

And at that moment I know where I am. I have been brought to witness the crucifixion. That was the purpose of the whole journey, and that is what I must do. But now I realize that I'm too close to see it. And so I have to push myself away from the beam and walk backwards from the cross in order to take in the scene before me, but this proves nearly impossible. My body seems made of lead. Whatever physical or moral strength I might once have had is gone. Nevertheless, somehow, after a terrible struggle, it is done.

But I still can't see the cross. It seems that my chin has fallen down upon my chest so that I can't see anything before me. If it was difficult to walk, to lift my head is more terrible still. It seems utterly impossible, and many times I think to give up trying. But at last that too is done.

And yet, still I cannot see the cross, for my eyes are closed. It is impossible to convey the difficulty of opening my eyes, so I will not try to describe it. I don't know how I did it, but in the end I did. And what I saw then, not twenty feet distant at the top of a small hillock, was indeed the crucifixion and the cross. But there was no body on it. *That* I could have borne to look at. To this day I still believe I could have looked at Jesus without trembling. But that was not what I saw. What I saw was a swirling cloud—a cloud upon a cross. And it was unbearable to look at. And yet I looked at it, because there was no power left anywhere within me to re-sist what I saw.

That was when I awoke. I was sitting bolt upright in my bed with my eyes open. I was crying and had been for quite a long time, because the front of the T-shirt I'd been sleeping in was completely drenched with tears. And at that moment lightning struck the oak tree in the yard by the river and split the trunk all the way to the ground.

I have never had a mystical vision, and I do not think that, as a mod-ern person, I could have endured this one while awake without ending up in a hospital somewhere, had I even survived it. In his mercy God gave it to me in something like a dream.

Even then, I could not speak for three days afterward. I would try and either no sound would come out, or only a few words spoken in a whis-per. I had no context apart from my rejected Christian upbringing for what had happened to me, and although I had lived for several years in Jacksonville by that time, I couldn't have told you the location of a single church. I tried to meditate, but it was impossible. I tried to remember what the voices had told me, but could recall none of it. Finally, I searched the works of Carl Jung and found in his writings a reference to something he called a "Great Dream," but he didn't say what to do in the event you actually had one. The gist of his advice seemed to be "You'll know."

I didn't. I didn't know what had happened to me and, as time went on, I came to feel vaguely resentful of what seemed an unwelcome Chris-tian incursion into what was by then shaping up to be a fine Zen life. So I pushed it to the back of my mind, where, as my Bible study partner would say, it became a "fishhook."

And that is what mothers are for.

There are moments in life when only a mother knows what's wrong with you and what to do about it, even if she doesn't always know how or why she knows. It was twenty years to the day when my mother called me from Oxford, Mississippi, where she and my father had retired a few years earlier. Somehow the subject of Jacksonville came up and she mentioned that she'd recently discovered a postcard I had sent her dated March 7, 1983, in which I'd referred to a dream of the night before, adding the cryptic Latin phrase *mysterium tremendum fascinans,* from the writings of Rudolf Otto, referring to the mix of ecstasy and terror one feels in the presence of the Living God. That dream—or rather, my failure to understand it—was what was wrong with me. And what to do about it turned out to be the study group I'd started with my friends. Even so it took years to unravel its meaning. When I did, I was stunned I hadn't understood before.

The words spoken by Jesus on the cross echo the opening verse of Psalm 22, where the speaker cries out to God from the depths of his own abandonment: "My God, my God, why hast thou forsaken me? why are thou so far from helping me, and from the words of my roaring?" Psalm 22 is striking for its use of crucifixion imagery, and for this reason it is regarded by most Christians as a prophecy, written hundreds of years before the event, of Jesus' death upon the cross.

Perhaps for this reason, Jesus' last words are rarely understood. Because Christians equate the psalm with a prophecy, they assume that in quoting from it, Jesus was speaking a kind of insider's shorthand—as if to say, "What is happening now is what was prophesied of the Messiah; therefore, I am he. I am that Messiah." But if that were the case—if Jesus were only indulging in an act of literary allusion—we could hardly feel moved by his words. No matter that they echo a beloved psalm, Jesus cries from the absolute depth of his own being as a mortal man when he utters them. That cry marks the furthest extremity of nothingness any human being can experience. At some point in life, any one of us may experience a moment when we feel we've lost it all—everything we ever loved or hoped or dreamed of—but we don't truly understand nothing-ness until we are lost from the presence of God.

The deepest paradox in all of the Bible is brought to the fore with Jesus' cry on the cross. For it is not only true, as all the great spiritual tra-ditions have taught, that the self must die in order for God to live within us, but that God *himself* must die. *All* our ideas must die in order for God to be born, even our idea of God. What few of us realize at the beginning of the spiritual journey is that what we call "God" is nearly always the self in disguise. We cry out to the cosmos and hear the echo of our own be-ing in return. Only when we reach the point of understanding that we are in the throes of that hallucinatory experience we call selfhood do we re-alize that we have made God in our own image, rather than the reverse. Only then do we understand what the mystics truly meant when they spoke of the death of the self. The death of God *is* the death of the self. And it is only out of that death that the experience of the One God can be born.

The problem is, when we put it this way, it sounds much too hard, like something only a mystic might achieve—and even then, only after a long sojourn in the desert, or maybe in Elijah's mountain cave. For the person living an ordinary life in the ordinary world, the death of the self is nearly inconceivable. "How will I survive?" we wonder. "How will I get through even the simplest tasks of any given day?" And, of course, those concerns would be realistic if by "death of the self" we meant the collapse of who we are on that ordinary, purely functional level. The truth taught by the Bible is that God dies *for* us, and through his death each one of us is brought to life.

Earlier this year, on a family vacation, we attended the Maundy Thursday service at the Church of the Good Shepherd in Wareham, Massachusetts. At the close of the service, my father-in-law, Matt Finn, rose from his seat to read Psalm 22, a liturgical exercise that ideally should have left the priest and his assistants enough time to strip the altar of all images, cloths, and texts in preparation for the Good Friday service the following day. Fortunately, they hadn't rehearsed it ahead of time, and that made all the difference.

As Matt reached the end of the psalm, the priest, his eight-year-old assistant, and various members of the Altar Guild were still going back and forth across the nave to remove all the various icons, books, and wall hangings. Then, just when it seemed to be over, the young girl remembered the bright red cushions on the seats to the left and right of the altar, and it took her three more trips to carry these. Finally, the cross itself was removed from the altar, and again everyone thought the ceremony was over. But then a member of the congregation whispered to the church warden that there was a sconce of flowers remaining just above the warden's head, and it took another minute to find a man from the choir who was tall enough to remove them. By now everyone was in on the act, myself included, scanning altar and nave to see if anything else remained. At that point, a member of the choir brought the cross, now draped in black for the Good Friday service, back out to put on the altar and things became momentarily confused. But the priest came back out and whispered, "No. Take it back inside."

And that was where it ended—with an altar temporarily left bare of all religious markers. The candles we had lit at the close of the service proper, passing the flame down each pew from hand to hand, were all blown out, and we left the church in silence, without so much as a single whisper—even from a child. And I was glad no one had thought to rehearse it. How do you rehearse nothingness? Best not even to try.

What does it mean to strip the altar of the heart so that nothing remains—not even the image of God? Isn't belief in God a process of removing everything from the heart *except* God? What could be the purpose of also removing God?

In the end, we really cannot imagine who or what God is. We cannot conceive of it. We can expand our minds with meditation, prayer, fasting, hallucinogenic drugs, or speaking in tongues, and it still isn't big enough. We can't contain the ocean in a thimble. We can't hold a galaxy in our hands. Even when we turn ourselves inside out, surrendering all that we called "me" and "mine" to the "thee" and "thine" of God, we *still* can't conceive of God. Surrender is not the same as grasping or understanding with the mind.

Even Jesus must endure the death of all his ideas about God, ideas that have come to him inevitably, just by virtue of his having been born with human faculties in an ordinary human form. That is why he cries out, "My God, my God, why hast thou forsaken me?"

Finally, that is what happens to Jesus on the cross, and the thing that must happen to us all. To experience the fullness of that Power Beyond the Self we call God, we must be willing to step beyond the self. We must be ready to remove all protective beliefs, images, and ideas from the altar of the heart and leave it empty.

But the simple reality of the matter is that we don't give up our false images of God until they fail us. When that happens, momentarily at least, we have no one and nothing to rely upon, and that is when we fall . . .

That is the reason why throughout history the collapse of traditional religious institutions has always boded well for the relationship between the individual seeker and God. God gets in through the cracks when our hearts and minds are broken. When our ideas about God are shattered, that is the moment God himself appears.

30

The Gateless Gate

And the twelve gates were twelve pearls: every several gate was
of one pearl: and the street of the city was pure gold, as it were
transparent glass. And I saw no temple therein: for the Lord God
Almighty and the Lamb are the temple of it.

—REVELATION 21:21–22

Anyone who has ever read the book of Revelation knows what a living
nightmare it is. No sooner have we begun to read it than we are con-
fronted with a world in the throes of death, disease, and every variety of
natural disaster known to man. And it is *our* world Revelation is talking
about, not some long-forgotten land of fairy tale or myth. For one thing,
the places it mentions still exist today. For another, its chaos and catas-
trophes are common in any age. Always there hovers about the limits of
human consciousness a nightmarish sense that some great moral reckoning is at hand. What most of us fail to realize is that God never intends
for us to remain in that nightmare. Like all bad dreams, we are meant to
emerge from it. The problem comes only when it proves impossible to
pinch ourselves awake.

Have you ever experienced a nightmare you couldn't wake from?
There is no way to describe the feeling of powerlessness and terror that

overwhelms us in those moments—the feeling of being pursued and unable to run, attacked and unable to call for help. At such moments we often scream, but can't seem to make a sound. We try to run, but our legs won't move. Something nameless looms over us, death is imminent, escape impossible. The nightmare is so compelling it completely displaces the waking world. We no longer remember who we are or where we live. We are lost from those who love us, the ones we might have turned to for help or comfort, or simply to tell us this isn't real.

Our nightmares are always seamless. However far we wander in that reality, it is always impossible to lift up a corner of it and see through to the other side. We *believe* in our nightmares, and nothing but waking can convince us otherwise. Even then, we often cry out when we finally emerge from them, their terrors seem so real. Our hearts are pounding, out breath comes out in gasps. Then slowly, at last, we begin to wake and know that the dangers and horrors we believed in just moments before were never actually real.

Like the terrifying dreams we all have from time to time, filled with obscure but strangely intimate symbols and portents, John's end-time scenario is compelling in every way. There is a universality to its portrait of the end of the world that makes it difficult to dismiss, even when nowadays we know that it was intended for first-century Christians, to inspire faith in the face of persecution, and is therefore written in a kind of symbolic code.

Some years ago Perdita and I were staying at the same hotel as a friend of ours, an internationally known environmental journalist. When the subject of my next book came up, his manner toward me suddenly changed and I was afraid that, like any number of our nonreligious friends, he'd taken offense at the title. Maybe he was afraid I'd try to talk him into believing in God, I thought, or maybe that I'd judge him for *not* believing. But that turned out not to be the case.

The next morning we met for breakfast at his suggestion, this time just the two of us, and even before the coffee had been poured, he leaned across the table and said with an urgency I found almost alarming, "Tell me about Revelation and what you think it means. Because I have to tell you, I'm beginning to believe it's real."

I could not have been more shocked had he told me that aliens had abducted his dog. Here was a person who lived and breathed on the cutting edge of science. True, he was a writer, like myself, and not a scientist per se. Nevertheless, science—*hard* science—was his stock-in-trade. It never occurred to me that he might have a religious bent, and it certainly never occurred to me that he might believe in end-time prophecy. But as our discussion continued, it all began to make sense.

Already at that point he was fully aware of the perils of global climate change. He'd read the science and seen the melting glaciers firsthand. He'd done the math, he assured me, and verified it with any number of climatologists around the world, and there was little room for doubt. Change was coming, probably much faster than anyone imagined, and he couldn't see how the news was going to be good.

So we talked about Revelation, and that was the first time I took it seriously—not as a book of specific prophecies that could be verified by looking at current events in the world, but as an end-time vision that made me realize the limits of the world we have created in our ongoing effort to displace the kingdom of God. Like our dreams, that world has its natural limits. Precisely because we have created it ourselves, it cannot endure for long.

Revelation offers a terrifying dream vision of hell on earth, replete with plagues and earthquakes, beasts and demons, not to mention oppression, abandonment, and war. But it is not a nightmare that God has created. We made it on our own. If there is any hope of waking from it, that hope lies in realizing this. Not that we can set the world to rights at this point without the help of God. But without understanding how we contribute to that nightmare, and how we keep ourselves asleep and dreaming it, there is little hope that anything will change.

Why do we do this? What causes us to sleep, and in our slumber to destroy the environment and one another, and finally even our sense of the world as a place to live and be? Why destroy the world that God created? Why can't we just wake up?

No one knows the answer to that question. God speaks to us from beyond our nightmare, often in the most intimate and loving terms, but the voice we *hear* is distorted by the story line of the dream we have created, which works according to the inexorable logic of a world created by the self. And so it often ends up sounding too judgmental to listen to. That modified voice tells us all sorts of things, some of them more terrifying than the dream itself, but the truth is, it is saying only the same thing over and over: *Child, wake up!* What we do for our own children when they are suffering needlessly is just what God does for us. But we have to be willing to let our nightmare go.

That is what the Buddha is trying to do for his disciples when he holds up a flower for all to see. And it is what Jesus is doing for his disciples when he tells them they are lilies of the field. The peace we seek does not lie any distance from where we are already. We just don't see it. We are too caught up in our dream.

Finally, there can be one thing only that keeps us from waking to the beauty and blessings of the world that God has made: our desire to be saved at the expense of our neighbor, interpreting that word *neighbor* in the broadest possible sense, to include not just human beings but every other flower of the field. This is what keeps us asleep and dreaming—the fact that we believe in a world with the self at its center, instead of the world created by God. The fact that we want that self to be saved *first*, that we want it to prevail or conquer, or simply for it to be right, not wrong. Call it tribalism, half-belief, or—bizarre as that paradox might seem—

even the instinct for survival, and it amounts to the same thing in the end: we want salvation for ourselves at the expense of the other, even if that other is the planet or humanity itself. To call this insane is an understatement. But, then, why should we be surprised? Has God not warned us of this from the very start? "For in the day thou eatest thereof thou shalt surely die."

There are, of course, some Christians who believe that they can escape the final reckoning through what they call the Rapture, being "caught up" by God at the last possible moment, leaving the rest of the world behind. But that notion itself is the cause of our nightmare. Let the Rapture come, it will make no difference. It is powerless to save us so long as the God we imagine is the god of few and not the God of All.

In the end, it all comes down to belief—*true* belief instead of half. And true belief comes to us only in the moment when the God we believe in is at last the God of everyone and everything. That is the meaning of the One God referred to in the Bible, and—spiritually speaking—it is all we have to learn in life. The rest of religion, with all its various customs (even customs disguised as belief), matters very little in the end. Religion, which can sometimes be a curse, can also be a cause for celebration when it is our way of coming to belief in God. But belief itself is never touched by religion. Belief lives only in the heart.

That One God is the reason why the book of Revelation, which seems such a despondent book throughout most of its twenty-two chapters, is so hopeful in the end. In the final two chapters of the Bible, which in every way mirror its *first* two chapters, a new heaven and earth are born—or, rather, the old heaven and earth are at last made visible to us again. They were there all along, but we weren't awake to them. In the end, nothing has changed, and everything has. What was impossible with men has, at last, been made possible by God.

That is the meaning of the vision John sees at the end of Revelation, after the stars have fallen, the moon has turned to blood, and the four horsemen have ridden their way to doom. The self awakens from its nightmare of global holocaust, and John sees the City of God, the New Jerusalem, descending upon earth from the heavens. And the first thing he notices about it, apart from its great size and splendor, is that it contains no temple: "For the Lord God Almighty and the Lamb [Jesus] are the temple of it. And the city had no need of the sun, neither of the moon, to shine in it: for the glory of God did lighten it, and the Lamb is the light thereof" (Revelation 21:22–23). We find further that the gates of that city are never shut, so that the glory and honor of every nation can enter freely into it. The gates of the New Jerusalem stand open because, in spite of the fact that its dimensions are essentially that of a giant cube, it is not a box. It *contains* nothing, but rather serves as a place of celebration, from which the joyful continually come and go. The city has no temple because God himself, the God of All, is finally living there.

For years the thing that intrigued me most about John's divine city was a detail that is seldom ever remarked upon: the fact that each of its twelve gates—three on each side—is comprised of a single pearl. I puzzled over this for a long time but couldn't understood how a pearl could be a gate, especially if it shut nothing and no one out. Finally, I looked to see if the Bible had said anything else about pearls, and it had.

Once when the disciples asked Jesus about the kingdom of heaven, he replied: "Again, the kingdom of heaven is like unto a merchant man, seeking goodly pearls: Who, when he had found one pearl of great price, went and sold all that he had, and bought it" (Matthew 13:45–46). *This* was the single, priceless pearl that guarded the gate to eternity. And that single pearl which stood at each of the twelve gates to the City of God was the One God himself. God himself was the doorway that stood forever wide, the gateless gate to eternity from which all things were forever arriving and departing, falling and being caught. And, just as Jesus had taught, it was worth everything you had to pay for it, because it *was* everything. The rest was only a dream.

APPENDIX A

Although the following summaries and explanations for each chapter of *How to Believe in God (Whether You Believe in Religion or Not)* may not be necessary for the reader who is familiar with the Bible, others may find them a helpful supplement to the text.

1: IN THE BEGINNING

Genesis is the first of the five books of the Hebrew Torah (often called the Pentateuch). The others are Exodus, Leviticus, Numbers, and Deuteronomy. The word *genesis* literally means "beginnings"; thus, the first book of the Bible relates the story, not only of the creation of the world, but of the beginnings of the Jewish people, explaining where they have come from and, through prophecies made by God to the first Jewish patriarchs and matriarchs, where they are going. The opening chapter of Genesis lays the basis for all of this by accounting for the creation of the physical universe out of an undifferentiated watery mass. To that end, God creates light on the first day, the sky on the second, the earth and all its vegetation on the third, and the sun, the moon, and the stars on the fourth. On the fifth day, God creates fish and birds, and on the sixth, the beasts of the field and, finally, human beings, commanding them to "be fruitful and multiply." The creation narrative comes to a close at the beginning of the second chapter of Genesis when God establishes the seventh day as the sabbath, or day of rest.

2: THE KNOWLEDGE OF GOOD AND EVIL

The origins of good and evil are explained by the Bible through the story of the first man and woman. Adam, whose name comes from the Hebrew word *adamah,* or "ground," is created when God fashions moist dust into a human form, breathing into its nostrils "the breath of life." Subsequently, Eve ("mother of life") is created from one of Adam's ribs while he is asleep. As their only guideline for life in the garden, God prohibits them from eating from the tree of knowledge of good and evil, telling them that they will die if they do.

The fall occurs as the result of a conversation between Eve and the serpent, the most "subtle" (or crafty) of all the creatures made by God. The serpent asks Eve if God has told her not to eat the fruit of any tree in the garden. Eve explains that they have been forbidden only from eating the fruit of the tree of knowledge. The serpent tells Eve that eating from the tree of knowledge will not kill her, but will enable her to discern good and evil and therefore be as wise as God.

Eve eats from the tree first, then offers the fruit to Adam, who also eats it, whereupon "their eyes were opened." Their first perception, however, is of their own nakedness, and their first act is to sew aprons of fig leaves to cover themselves. Afterward, they hide.

When God asks Adam why he is hiding, Adam explains that he is naked. God asks if they have eaten from the tree of knowledge, and Adam answers that Eve has given him fruit. Eve tells God that the serpent is to blame for deceiving her, for which deception God curses the serpent to crawl on his belly and makes humanity his perpetual enemy. Eve is condemned to suffer pain in childbirth and placed under the dominion of her husband, while Adam is condemned to life as a farmer. The ground will no longer yield its fruit to him without great effort. Therefore life will be a perpetual struggle for survival.

At last God makes clothes for Adam and Eve from the skins of animals, and they are expelled from the garden. To prevent them from returning and seeking to attain immortality, God places an angel with a flaming sword at the gate of Eden to guard the way to the tree of life.

3: CAIN AND ABEL

After leaving the garden, Eve bears Cain, a tiller of the ground, and then Abel, a keeper of sheep. In the Bible's first recorded offering before God, Cain offers the fruit of the ground, while his brother Abel brings the first-born of his flock, including their "fat portions."

When God shows preference for Abel's offering over Cain's, Cain is angry and "his countenance falls." God asks why he is so upset, and when Cain offers no reply, adds, "Will you not be accepted if you do well?" Then he warns Cain, "If you do not do well, sin is lurking at the door; its desire is for you, but you must master it."

Soon after, Cain lures his brother Abel into the field and slays him. The Lord asks Cain where his brother is, and Cain replies, "Am I my brother's keeper?" God tells Cain that the land will no longer support him as a farmer and he is therefore cursed to be a wanderer. His tongue loosened at last, Cain confesses that his punishment is more than he can bear. Having killed his brother, he now fears that anyone who meets him will seek to kill him as well. But God shows mercy, placing a mark on Cain's forehead so that anyone who meets him will be warned that, if they harm him, they will be punished seven times over. Cain leaves the area just outside of Eden where he has been living with his parents and journeys to the land of Nod. There he marries and becomes father to Enoch, who builds the first city. Because Eve has lost

Abel, and because Cain has been exiled, God gives her another son, named Seth.

4: THE UNFINISHED TOWER

Having survived the flood, the descendants of Noah gather on the plains of Shinar to build a great city with a tower that will reach into the heavens so that "they might make a name for themselves and not be scattered over the earth." The people bake durable bricks for that purpose and likewise fashion mortar from bitumen (the first mention of such technology in the Bible). The Lord comes down with his angels to see what work the people of Babel are about and concludes that, because they are a unified people who all speak the same language, nothing will be beyond their power. Together with his angels, God confuses their speech so that they can no longer work cooperatively on the tower and scatters them over the face of the earth. For this reason, the Bible tells, the city came to be known as Babel, meaning "confusion."

5: GOING FORTH

Abram is the first patriarch of Judaism and Islam, through his sons Isaac and Ishmael, respectively. Told by God to go forth to a new land, he departs at once from Haran with his wife, Sarah, his brother's son Lot, and all of their servants. God leads Abram and his family on various journeys through what is now Syria, Lebanon, Israel, and Egypt, and promises to make his descendants as numerous as the stars of the sky, whereupon he is renamed Abraham, "the father of many." Famous episodes involving Abraham include his attempt to intercede with God on behalf of the doomed cities of Sodom and Gomorrah and his near sacrifice of his son Isaac. He dies at the age of 175 and is carried by his sons to Hebron, where he is buried in the Cave of Machpelah.

6: THE BINDING OF ISAAC

When Abraham is told that he will father a great nation, he wonders how this can be accomplished since he has no children and his wife is very old. In order to produce an heir, Sarah convinces Abraham to conceive a child with her handmaid, Hagar. Thus, Ishmael is born. When Sarah later over-hears an angel say that she too will bear a son, she laughs, but soon after, at the age of ninety, she bears Isaac. Now that Sarah has produced a legit-imate heir, she sends Hagar away. God promises that both of Abraham's sons will produce great nations but maintains the sanctity of his covenant with Abraham through the child born of his legitimate wife, Sarah.

Abruptly, in chapter 22 of Genesis, we are told that God decided to test Abraham by requiring him to sacrifice his son. Abraham, who ear-lier argued with God against the destruction of Sodom and Gomorrah, makes no protest here, but quickly gathers his son, his two servants, and wood for the burnt offering and departs for the mountain God has told him about. At no point in the story does he question God's motives or show any emotion whatsoever. We know only that, just as Abraham is about to sacrifice his son, an angel intervenes. Abraham looks up to see a ram with its horns caught in a thicket and offers that instead. How does he feel about the test? Does he know that it is a test? How does he feel afterward about what has happened? The story itself offers no an-swer to what is considered by some the most puzzling episode in all of the Bible.

7: JACOB AND THE ANGEL

When Isaac's wife, Rebecca, is pregnant, she experiences great discomfort and calls upon the Lord for guidance. God tells her that two great nations are at war within her womb and that the elder will serve the younger. When the twins Jacob and Esau are born, Esau emerges from the womb first, with his brother grasping him by the heel, hence the name Jacob, "heel grasper." As the brothers grow up, Esau becomes an outdoorsman and a hunter, while Jacob, more thoughtful by nature, is content staying home in the tent.

In an episode that prefigures events between the two brothers, Esau returns from the hunt one day nearly starved, and Jacob, who has been cooking some red lentil stew, offers him a bowl of it in exchange for his birthright. The fact that Esau accepts may have been intended to confirm what God has already told Rebecca: that Jacob will receive the blessing rather than Esau, who may be seen not to deserve it, since he is willing to sell it so cheaply.

When the time comes for Isaac to pass God's blessing to Esau, Jacob receives the blessing instead because of a deception invented by Rebecca. Jacob will impersonate his brother, who is quite hairy, by tying goatskins to his arms and wearing his brother's clothes. Isaac has now become quite blind and so, although he is suspicious, noting that his son doesn't sound like himself, he nevertheless accepts Jacob's claim to be his brother Esau and offers him God's blessing and all of the power, possessions, and prosperity that accompany it. When Esau discovers what his brother has done, he vows to kill him, whereupon Rebecca sends Jacob off to live with his Uncle Laban.

Jacob passes many years with Laban in Padan-aram. He marries both of Laban's daughters (Rachel, whom he loves, and Leah, whom he does not) and eventually becomes even more wealthy than his uncle. At that time, God tells Jacob that it is time to return home to the land of his ancestors. It is on this journey that he wrestles with the angel.

8: THE NAME OF GOD

Moses is born of a Jewish mother at a time when the Jews, now enslaved, are becoming numerous in Egypt. In an effort to reduce their numbers,

Pharaoh commands that all male babies be drowned. Fearing this fate for her child, Moses' mother sets him adrift in a basket on the Nile, where Pharaoh's own daughter finds him, giving him the name Moses, meaning "drawn from water," and raising him as her own.

When he is a young man, Moses sees an Egyptian foreman beating one of his Jewish kinsmen and kills the Egyptian. To escape punishment for his crime, he journeys to Midian, where he marries Zipporah and works for her father as a shepherd. It is while wandering with his flock that Moses comes upon the burning bush and is given the task of liberating the Israelites from slavery. Unsure of his fitness for this mission, Moses tries a variety of stratagems to wiggle out of it, but in the end God prevails and Moses confronts Pharaoh with his demands.

Pharaoh refuses to let the Israelites leave, and Moses brings down ten plagues upon the house of Egypt, finally winning freedom for his people when God sends the angel of death to take the firstborn child from each Egyptian household, as well as the firstborn animals and livestock. With this final plague, at last Pharaoh relents and the people are freed. He changes his mind, however, once the Israelites have departed and pursues them as far as the Red Sea. Moses uses his staff to part the sea for the Israelites, but the waters come crashing back once the Egyptians try to pursue them, and Pharaoh's army is drowned.

Following their successful deliverance, the Israelites are led through the Sinai Desert for forty years, during which time they learn how to behave as God's people. They are allowed to enter the Promised Land only when this process is complete.

9: THE GOLDEN CALF

The episode in which the Israelites fashion a golden calf occurs just as Moses is preparing to come down from Mount Sinai with the tablets of the law. A full discussion of this act of idolatry and what motivates it can be found in Chapter 9. The aftermath of that event, however, is little known.

Once the calf has been destroyed (Moses has its gold ground to powder and mixed with water that the offenders are required to drink), a bloodbath ensues, led by the Levites, the priestly tribe of Israel. Moses commands these priests to strap their swords upon their thighs and to go throughout the camp killing their brothers, friends, and neighbors, until about three thousand people lie dead. In this way, Moses tells the Levites, they have ordained themselves for the service of the Lord, "each one at the cost of a son or a brother, and so have brought a blessing on yourselves this day." The next day Moses reminds the people that they have committed a great sin but promises that he will intercede with God on their behalf. At Moses' urging, God spares the lives of the Israelites and sends a plague upon them instead.

10: THE DEATH OF MOSES

Moses' death before he has an opportunity to reach the Promised Land is one of the great disappointments in the Bible. The punishment hinges upon what would seem a minor lapse.

When the Israelites are thirsty, God commands Moses to strike a stone with his staff, whereupon water gushes out. Again, when the Israelites are thirsty, Moses does the same. Only this time he takes credit for the miracle, along with his brother Aaron. For this sin, God tells him, he will never reach the Promised Land alive. When the forty years of wandering are at an end, God takes him to the top of Mount Pisgah, where he is allowed to see the Promised Land, after which he dies "according to the word of the Lord," who buries him in secret. The Torah ends with a series of verses reminiscent of the heroic literature of the ancient world, suggesting that, despite what seems to be a harsh decree against him, Moses is nevertheless regarded as the greatest prophet in the history of Israel:

And there arose not a prophet since in Israel like unto Moses,
whom the Lord knew face to face, In all the signs and the wonders,
which the Lord sent him to do in the land of Egypt to Pharaoh,
and to all his servants, and to all his land, And in all that mighty
hand, and in all the great terror which Moses shewed in the sight
of all Israel.

(DEUTERONOMY 34:10–12)

11: HANNAH'S PRAYER

Elkanah, a Levite, has two wives, Hannah and Peninnah. But while Peninnah has children, Hannah does not, because "the Lord had closed her womb." Ridiculed for her infertility by her rival, Hannah is so distraught that she eventually stops eating. Elkanah insists that she should be satisfied with his love (he prefers her over Peninnah), but she is not consoled. Presenting herself in all her misery at the tabernacle in Shiloh, Hannah prays ardently for a male child.

And she vowed a vow, and said, O Lord of hosts, if thou wilt indeed
look on the affliction of thine handmaid, and remember me, and
not forget thine handmaid, but wilt give unto thine handmaid a
man child, then I will give him unto the Lord all the days of his life,
and there shall no razor come upon his head.

(1 SAMUEL 1:11)

Because Hannah prays silently, moving only her lips, the chief priest Eli believes she is intoxicated and rebukes her, only to be told that she has not taken in spirits but rather has done the opposite, pouring *out* her spirit before the Lord. Hearing this, Eli is deeply moved and blesses Hannah, assuring her that God will hear such a prayer. Hannah returns to her husband and begins to eat again. Upon returning home she conceives the child, Samuel, who becomes a prophet to the first two kings of Israel, Saul and David.

12: FIVE SMOOTH STONES

The Israelites are at war against the Philistines. David's father, Jesse, calls him in from the pastures where he has been tending his flocks and tells him to take some provisions to his older brothers, who are fighting in the war. David does so, but when he arrives at the Israelite camp, he finds morale very low. A great giant of a man, one Goliath of Gath, has taken it upon himself to taunt the Israelites each day with the following challenge: if any among them is strong enough to defeat him in single combat, the Philistines will become their slaves. If, however, Goliath wins the contest, then the Israelites will become *their* slaves. Judging from his prowess in battle, and the sheer bulk of his physical size (we are told that Goliath is around ten feet all), he must be reasonably confident that no one will take the risk. His challenge is meant to humiliate them.

David asks what will be done for the man who defeats the giant and is told that King Saul will make such a man rich and give him his daughter in marriage. With this knowledge the boy David decides to fight the giant. To the incredulous King Saul, he explains that in the past the Lord has helped him prevail against a lion and a bear who came to attack his flock. Admittedly, Goliath is a different kind of challenge, but God will help him to prevail.

Saul thinks that the young boy will surely die in battle against a seasoned soldier such as Goliath, but as there seems to be no one else willing to take up the challenge, he allows David to do battle. As David is about to leave, Saul offers him his armor. David tries it on but, because he's not used to it, decides it's better to leave it behind. He stops at the brook to choose five stones for his sling and then goes forth to meet the Philistine with only his sling and his shepherd's staff in his hand.

The battle commences with ritual taunting. Seeing David armed only with his shepherd's tools, Goliath cries out, "Am I a dog, that thou comest to me with staves?" Whereupon David replies:

> *Thou comest to me with a sword, and with a spear, and with a shield: but I come to thee in the name of the Lord of hosts, the God of the armies of Israel, whom thou hast defied. This day will the Lord deliver thee into mine hand; and I will smite thee, and take thine head from thee.*
>
> (1 SAMUEL 17:45–46)

With this, Goliath approaches the shepherd boy, who puts a stone into his sling and hurls it at the giant. The stone strikes Goliath, sinking into his forehead, and he falls dead facedown on the ground. David grasps the giant's sword and cuts off his head, and the Philistines flee as the Israelites pursue them.

13: DAVID DANCES BEFORE THE ARK

The Ark of the Covenant was built during Moses' lifetime in accordance with instructions provided by God. Made to house the tablets of the law, it was considered the holiest object in all of Israel. Later, when David's son, Solomon, built the temple at Jerusalem, it occupied the "Holiest of Holies," the inner sanctum, where it was visited once each year on Yom Kippur by the head priest.

Considered a very powerful object, it was sometimes carried into battle. Thus it came to fall into the hands of the Philistines, when they defeated the army of Israel.

The Philistines did not fare well with the ark, however. It caused the idol in the temple at Ashdod to fall over and its hands and feet to fall off. It then caused the people to develop tumors. The Philistines tried moving it to Gath, but the same illnesses occurred. When the ark was moved to Ekron with the same results, the people there rejected it, and it was returned to Israel. There it abided at the home of Abinadab. This is where David finds it.

Seen in light of this longer history, the death of Uzzah, who dies because he "put forth his hand" to steady the ark when the oxen stumbled, seems consistent with the overall impression created by the Bible that the ark is a holy, but also a dangerous thing. It is only later, when King David discovers in the Torah the rules governing the proper handling of the ark, that it can be safely moved to Jerusalem.

About the matter of David's dancing as the ark is being brought into the city, the Bible tells us that his wife Michal, Saul's daughter, was offended that the king of Israel should be seen dancing in his loincloth before serving maids. David replies that it is enough to be honored by the serving maids of Israel. Thereafter he rejects her and she dies childless.

14: A HANDFUL OF MEAL

Elijah the Tishbite was an important prophet to the Northern Kingdom of Israel during the ninth century B.C.E. Nothing is known of his life before the moment he appears on the scene, already a prophet, telling King Ahab that, as God's punishment for the sin of idolatry, it will not rain for many years. A vigorous man able to endure long sojourns in the wilderness, Elijah lives for a time near a brook in Jordan where he is fed by ravens. Later, God commands him to travel to Zarephath, where a widow will provide him with food. The widow and her son are starving, but Elijah intervenes and her meager store of food and oil are prolonged until the end of the drought. When her son later succumbs to illness, Elijah prays that he be revived, and he is resurrected from the dead. Afterward, the widow tells Elijah, "Now by this I know that thou art a man of God, and that the word of the Lord in thy mouth is truth."

15: ELIJAH PRAYS FOR RAIN

Elijah's prayer to end the drought is preceded by a contest with the prophets of Baal. Elijah begins by rebuking the people of Israel for the indecisiveness of their religious beliefs: "How long halt ye between two opinions? if the Lord be God, follow him: if Baal, then follow him" (1 Kings 18:21). When the people remain silent, Elijah proposes a test. Each side will offer a sacrifice, only without using fire. Whichever god is able to produce fire to burn the offering will then command the loyalty of the people.

The prophets of Baal (some 450 in number) offer their prayer first, dancing and invoking his name, and even slashing themselves with knives, but to no avail. Elijah mocks their efforts, suggesting that Baal must be sleeping. Elijah then commands that four barrels of water be poured over the wood below his own offering, drenching it thoroughly. This process is repeated twice more, after which, even with that handicap, Elijah's prayer immediately produces a fire that consumes not only the sacrifice but the stones beneath it. Baal's prophets are then slain by the people of Israel, a deed that later inspires Queen Jezebel to seek Elijah's death.

Immediately following this very public encounter, Elijah retreats to Mount Carmel with his servant to pray for rain. The pose Elijah takes, placing his head between his knees, suggests that he has entered deep meditation. He emerges from this state only at intervals to send his servant to the top of the mountain to look out at the sea. At first the servant sees nothing. Finally, on the seventh ascent, he spies a cloud the size of a man's hand. Elijah accepts this as the sign that he has been waiting for and, indeed, the sky is soon thick with clouds. With the end of idolatry, the drought ends also, and Elijah rushes back to the city ahead of King Ahab with the wind pushing at his back.

16: A STILL SMALL VOICE

Pursued by the vengeful Queen Jezebel, Elijah flees to Mount Horeb (a journey of forty days) and secrets himself inside a cave. There he hears the voice of the Lord asking why he is hiding. Elijah answers that the prophets of Israel have all been slain and that only he is left. Now Jezebel has sworn to kill him, too, and there seems no hope for the future of his mission. Elijah is told to walk toward the entrance of the cave. There he witnesses a series of three revelations:

> And, behold, the Lord passed by, and a great and strong wind rent
> the mountains, and brake in pieces the rocks before the Lord; but
> the Lord was not in the wind: and after the wind an earthquake;
> but the Lord was not in the earthquake: And after the earthquake
> a fire; but the Lord was not in the fire.
>
> (1 KINGS 19:11–12)

Then comes "a still small voice." Elijah steps outside the entrance of the cave when he hears it, pulling his cloak up over his head so that he will not risk seeing God's face, which was forbidden even to Moses. As he stands there, God asks him the same question as before and receives the same answer from Elijah: the prophets are all dead and only he is left.

God tells Elijah to journey to Damascus and anoint Hazael as king of Syria and Jehu as king of Israel. He is then to anoint Elisha as his successor.

When the time comes for Elijah to die, he is taken up into heaven in a chariot of fire right before Elisha's eyes. Only his cloak floats down from the heavens. Elisha takes up Elijah's mantle (quite literally) and parts the Jordan by smiting the waters with it, the first of many miracles this new prophet will perform in the Bible.

17: QUESTIONING GOD

The book of Job tells the story of a man who suffers the loss of his home, his children, his wealth, and even his health—all through no fault of his own. The main story begins with a conversation in heaven between God and Satan.

God asks where Satan has just come from, and Satan replies: "From going to and fro in the earth, and from walking up and down in it."

"Hast thou considered my servant Job," says God, "that there is none like him in the earth, a perfect and an upright man, one that feareth God, and escheweth evil?" (Job 1:7–8)

Satan replies that, indeed, he has noticed Job, but adds that Job can hardly have any reason to fear God, since God has given him unrivaled prosperity and protection. Satan dares God to test Job by taking away everything he has, confident that Job will then curse him to his face. God gives Satan permission to administer such a test, but makes him promise not to harm Job himself. The scene shifts to earth, where a series of messengers arrives to tell Job that his livestock have all been stolen or destroyed and that his sons and daughters have perished when their house collapsed. Job mourns these losses but ultimately accepts his misfortune as the inscrutable will of an all-powerful God.

God feels vindicated in the observation he has made earlier that Job is "a perfect and an upright man," and says as much to Satan. But Satan is not so easily defeated. Job will surely curse God if he is directly afflicted himself. God gives his permission for such a test, provided Satan does not take Job's life. This is how Job comes to be alone, seated on an ash heap, his entire body, including the soles of his feet, covered with painful boils. It is in this condition that his three friends find him.

The bulk of Job's forty-two chapters concerns his conversation with these friends, who seem concerned not just about Job's suffering but also about its implications for the rest of humanity. At first they are empathetic and respectful of his sorrow, but their responses become increasingly moralistic and theologically abstruse. In his grief and suffering, Job's responses to his friends range from despair to moral outrage, since he alone knows that he is completely blameless and therefore does not deserve to suffer at the hands of the Lord.

Finally, Job demands and receives an audience with God, who speaks to him out of a whirlwind, asking a series of questions that spans the breadth and depth of the cosmos, inquiring of Job whether he knows if the rain has a father, or out of whose womb the ice comes forth. Where was Job when the foundation of the earth was laid? Does Job give the horse its might? Is it at Job's command that the eagle takes flight and makes its nest on high? If Job cannot answer even one of these questions, how can God answer the question of why Job suffers?

In the end, it is God himself who is the answer to Job's question. And when Job relents in the face of such majesty and power, God gives back his health and possessions and many more children besides. In the Hebrew original all of this is told in poetry whose language is terrifying and beautiful, mystical and inspirational in turn.

18: THE TWO WAYS

The Psalms have been called "the prayer book of Israel," but that designation is misleading for the modern reader, because few prayer books today contain the range and variety of expression to be found in the 150 poems that compose the Psalms.

It has long been observed that one can find every imaginable human emotion or predicament in the Psalms, and every mode of expression, too. For if the Psalms contain many laments, they contain joyous odes as well. If there are more than a few battle hymns among their number, there we also find the comforting sweetness of the "shepherd's psalm." On occasion the Psalms even give voice to something like the mood of existential despair and alienation so prevalent in modern life: "I watch [lie awake], and am as a sparrow alone upon the house top" (Psalm 102:7). In all, the Psalms might be said to offer a portrait of humanity; specifically, they record the meditations (literally, the "mutterings") of a people long dead whose lives, though different from our own in most outward respects, were governed by the same human cares and concerns.

The authorship of the Psalms is traditionally ascribed to King David. The truth seems to be that they were written by diverse individuals, responding to a wide variety of conditions, over a period of perhaps a thousand years.

19: THE WAKEFUL HEART

The Song of Songs (sometimes known by the title "Song of Solomon" or "Canticles") was probably inspired by an older tradition of Middle Eastern love poems designed to be sung at weddings or banquets. Jewish records indicate that the Song may still have been used for this purpose as late as the second century C.E. By that time the Song may have been associated with the harvest festival, a time when young women would frequently visit the fields outside Jerusalem in an attempt to attract the notice of suitors. By then, however, Jewish rabbis had already begun to read the Song of Songs as an allegory of love between God and Israel, and that is doubtless how it came to be included among the liturgical readings for the celebration of Passover, even though there are no explicit religious references to be found in it, and God's name is never mentioned.

The Song of Songs is traditionally associated with King Solomon, David's son, but it seems more likely that it is the culmination of an oral tradition of Middle Eastern love poetry and is therefore a poem of uncertain authorship.

20: JONAH AND THE VINE

God speaks to the prophet Jonah, commanding him to journey to the Assyrian city of Nineveh and warn its people to abandon their wicked ways. However, Jonah has no desire to save the Ninevites, historically the enemies of Israel. Instead of journeying to Nineveh, he travels in the opposite direction, boarding a ship for Tarshish. A great storm overtakes the ship, and when the sailors cast lots to determine who has found disfavor with his god, the lot falls on Jonah, who is sound asleep in the hold. They wake him and he proposes that as a solution they cast him into the sea. Although reluctant to do so, the sailors decide they have no choice and throw Jonah overboard.

The Lord sends a great fish (nowhere does it say a whale), which swallows Jonah. There he remains for three days and nights. At last he relents and agrees to do God's bidding. The fish spits Jonah out on the shore, and this time when the Lord commands him to Nineveh, he goes. Nineveh is so large a city that it takes Jonah three days to walk from one end of it to the other. He does so, proclaiming all the while God's plan to destroy the city if its people do not repent. In what is surely the most successful act of prophecy in the Bible, the inhabitants of Nineveh, from the king down to the animals in the fields, immediately don sackcloth and repent their evil ways. Jonah alone is disappointed by this development. He begs God to take his life rather than leave him to watch the deliverance of the Ninevites, but God asks only, "Doest thou well to be angry?"

Jonah builds a temporary shelter to the east of Nineveh and waits to see what will become of the city. To shade him from the sun, the Lord causes a gourd vine to grow up over his head. But on the next day the Lord sends a worm to destroy the vine and, when Jonah mourns the loss of the vine and once more wishes he were dead, again the Lord asks, "Doest thou well to be angry for the gourd?" Jonah replies that he is right to be angry, angry even unto death.

This must have been what the Lord suspected, for in the end he asks Jonah, "And should not I spare Nineveh, that great city, wherein are more than sixscore thousand persons that cannot discern between their right hand and their left hand; and also much cattle?" The question is probably rhetorical, because Jonah offers no answer. It is here the story ends.

21: JESUS HOLDS UP A FLOWER

The Sermon on the Mount, which takes place over three chapters (Matthew 5–7), is not only the first sustained period of teaching by Jesus in the Bible, containing many of his most important teachings, including the Beatitudes and the Lord's Prayer, it is also the longest. No summary can do justice to the Sermon's perfection as a spiritual teaching, but it is worth noting two general features about its content and one about its setting.

The first is that the Sermon offers a reinterpretation of Jewish law. For while the Torah teaches that one must not commit murder, Jesus tells his disciples that they will be judged even if they only harbor grudges or fail to make peace with their neighbor. Similarly, the law teaches parity (that it is just to take an eye for an eye and a tooth for a tooth), while Jesus teaches that real fairness is achieved only by treating others as we ourselves would wish to be treated. Thus, he tells his disciples to love even their enemies and to pray for them.

Second is the fact that Jesus favors the internalization of the law over its outward observance. Thus he advises us to pray in private and give alms anonymously rather than making a public display of either, for it is more important that God know what is in our hearts than that we be praised by others for only seeming to be religious.

Finally, at a time when Jewish religious life is still centered upon the temple at Jerusalem, the fact that the Sermon is delivered out of doors in a remote setting roots its teaching in the life of the country rather than the life of the city. The impulse to travel into the wilderness or climb a mountain, to get away from it all and to rise above the hubbub and distractions of daily life, is itself a fundamentally religious impulse in the sense that it restores religion, which is apt to be coopted by the collective, to the realm of individual experience.

The forty-year desert wanderings of the people of Israel can be seen in this light, as can Moses' ascent of Mount Sinai. The people of Israel, having become enslaved not simply by the Egyptians but, in a deeper sense, by Egyptian culture, journey to Sinai to recover their religious impulse. In a similar way, Jesus leads his disciples and other followers through the countryside and finally up a mountain where he delivers a sermon that restores the religion of Israel to itself. To understand the message of the Sermon, it is essential to read it in this light. It was delivered to a people who, symbolically at least, had found themselves in Egypt once again, in a culture that defined their experience in collective terms. It was a way of recentering the religious impulse in the life of the individual believer.

22: THE EVIL PERSON

Upon encountering some "which trusted in themselves that they were righteous, and despised others" Jesus tells the parable of two men who go up to the temple to pray on the same occasion. One is a Pharisee (from the Hebrew word "to separate"), a member of a Jewish sect concerned with matters of purity and the correct observance of Jewish law. The other is a publican, or tax collector. The Pharisee declares to God that he has not committed acts of extortion or adultery, but rather has fasted and paid his tithes (literally, "a tenth" of his income, as prescribed by Jewish law). He contrasts himself with the publican, a sinner and a Roman collaborator, thanking God that he is not like him.

The publican is a sinner and confesses as much before God, too ashamed even to look up toward heaven. Jesus concludes: "I tell you, this man [the publican] went down to his house justified rather than the other [the Pharisee]: for every one that exalteth himself shall be abased; and he that humbleth himself shall be exalted."

23: LOST AND FOUND

When he is criticized for associating with sinners and publicans, Jesus responds with a series of three parables meant to show how God cares especially for those who find themselves lost or alone.

In the parable of the lost sheep, God is compared to a shepherd. "What man of you, having an hundred sheep, if he lose one of them, doth not leave the ninety and the nine in the wilderness, and go after that which is lost, until he find it?" asks Jesus. For people living at a time when livestock played an essential role in daily life, the question must surely have been rhetorical. Any good shepherd would search for the sheep that had become lost.

In the parable of the lost coin, Jesus compares God to a woman who has lost a precious silver drachma and immediately lights a candle and sets about sweeping the entire house until it has been found. The implication is that, though he or she may feel unworthy, the lost soul is nevertheless a great treasure in God's eyes.

Finally, Jesus offers one of his most famous parables, the story of the prodigal son. In this parable God is the father of two sons. One son follows all the rules of propriety and expects to be rewarded for his good behavior. The other lives riotously and loses all of his money, eventually becoming a penniless wanderer. Thinking that even the hired servants in his father's fields have bread enough to spare, the boy returns home, no longer expecting to be treated as a son but willing to work as a laborer. The father, who has been waiting anxiously, sees him coming from afar and runs out to embrace him. He dresses the boy in his best robe, puts shoes on his feet, and commands that the fatted calf be killed for a celebratory feast. The parable ends with the other son protesting that his father has never "killed the fatted calf" for him, although he has always been more responsible than his brother. But the father only answers that he had thought the younger son was dead, and now he has been found alive. How can he do anything but rejoice with all his heart?

24: FORGIVENESS

The Lord's Prayer, also known as the "Our Father," after its opening words, appears in two versions in the Gospels. The first occurs in Matthew 6 during the Sermon on the Mount, the second in Luke 11. Matthew's version is the one traditionally used in Christian liturgy and is therefore the version best known today:

> *Our Father, which art in heaven, Hallowed be thy name.*
> *Thy kingdom come. Thy will be done in earth, as it is in heaven.*
> *Give us this day our daily bread.*
> *And forgive us our debts, as we forgive our debtors.*
> *And lead us not into temptation, but deliver us from evil:*
> *For thine is the kingdom, and the power, and the glory, for ever.*
> *Amen.*

It should be noted that the passage beginning "For thine is the kingdom" does not appear in many early manuscripts of the gospels. This doxology (formula of "praise") was added later in recognition of the prayer's widespread use in Christian liturgy and private devotion.

Traditionally, the Lord's Prayer is said to contain seven petitions: (1) for the "hallowing" of God's name (i.e., for an attitude of reverence toward it), (2) for the coming of his kingdom, (3) for the uniting of this world with the heavenly world by submission to the will of God, (4) for food and other indispensable provisions of daily life, (5) for forgiveness, (6) for deliverance from circumstances that would lead to temptation, and (7) for deliverance from evil.

In Matthew, the Lord's Prayer is followed by Jesus' teaching on the importance of forgiving others. In Luke, he follows the prayer with an analogy comparing God to a friend who would surely get up in the middle of the night to give bread to his neighbor simply because he had asked for it.

25: A NEW BIRTH

Nicodemus is described in the Bible as a Pharisee and a teacher of the Jews. He appears three times in the Gospel of John: in chapter 3 he comes under cover of night to ask Jesus how a man can be born when he is old; in 7 he questions the council's justice in condemning Jesus before they have heard his defense; and in 19, at considerable risk to himself, he publicly assists Joseph of Arimathea with Jesus' burial. Only in the first encounter, however, does Nicodemus emerge as a developed character.

Nicodemus arrives at night because he is reluctant to be seen with Jesus during the daytime. He begins by remarking on the miracles that Jesus has performed and concludes that he must have been sent by God. Nicodemus is troubled by the implications of this, however, since Jesus' teachings are at variance with those of the Pharisees on many points.

In reply, Jesus tells Nicodemus that he must be born again to see the kingdom of God. Unsure whether to interpret this literally or not, Nicodemus asks if a man can enter a second time into his mother's womb. Again, Jesus insists that he must be born again. He then describes that experience for Nicodemus by comparing it to a wind that you can hear the sound of, even though you cannot tell where it comes from or where it is going.

Nothing further is said of Nicodemus in this first episode, but his subsequent behavior has suggested to later Christians that he was, like Joseph of Arimathea, a secret disciple of Jesus.

26: THE MORAL CENTER

The story of the woman taken in adultery does not appear in early manuscripts of the Gospel of John. This, and the fact that no Greek church father comments on the story before the twelfth century, has led most modern scholars to question its authenticity, although some believe that it may have been part of an older oral tradition. At this late date, however, the episode is so well loved that its place in the biblical canon is no longer negotiable. Nevertheless, most modern translations include a note questioning its origin.

According to the story that has come down to us, Jesus is teaching at the temple in Jerusalem one morning when the scribes and Pharisees present him with a woman who has been caught in the act of adultery. Given that, the man must have been caught as well, but they have neglected to bring him along. In asking Jesus to decide the matter of her punishment, the woman's accusers present him with a clever trap. Jews are forbidden under Roman law from administering the death penalty; at the same time, if he neglects the woman's sin, he will lose credibility as a teacher in the eyes of Israel. In overlooking the fundamental spirit of the law, however, which is to inspire repentance and self-reflection, they have left themselves open to an interpretation that defeats them all.

Under Jewish law only those who were not guilty of the same sin could administer punishment. Glancing about him, Jesus wisely guesses that the woman's accusers are themselves guilty (either in fact or in their hearts) of the same sin, and so he demands of them, "He that is without sin among you, let him first cast a stone at her." Hearing this, they all disappear. Jesus, who alone could rightfully administer her punishment, asks the woman, "Where are those thine accusers?" And she replies that they have gone. "Neither do I condemn thee: go, and sin no more," he tells her, bringing the matter to a close.

27: THE NEEDLE'S EYE

The story of the rich young ruler appears in three gospels. As Jesus is passing by on the road, a young man recognizes him as the rabbi from Galilee and runs after him to ask a burning question: what must he do to inherit eternal life?

Jesus tells him to follow the commandments—not to commit adultery, not to murder, not to steal, not to bear false witness—but the young man declares that he has followed these all of his life. Hearing this, Jesus decides to invite him to become a disciple: "One thing thou lackest: go thy way, sell whatsoever thou hast, and give to the poor, and thou shalt have treasure in heaven: and come, take up the cross, and follow me." Unable to part with his wealth, the young man walks away in sorrow.

This gives rise to one of Jesus' most famous pronouncements: "It is easier for a camel to go through the eye of a needle, than for a rich man to enter into the kingdom of God." On hearing this, the disciples are momentarily at a loss, asking, "Who then can be saved?" But Jesus explains that while men are unable to save themselves, salvation is nevertheless still possible because of God, "for with God all things are possible."

28: THE SIGN OF THE KISS

Judas Iscariot's surname implies that he may have been born in Kerioth, a town in southern Palestine, which would make him the only non-Galilean among the twelve disciples. The gospels all agree that he is the betrayer of Jesus, although in Mark this is not stated directly but must be inferred.

On the night before the crucifixion, Judas meets with the chief priests, accepting thirty pieces of silver in exchange for betraying Jesus' location and agreeing to identify him with a kiss when the soldiers arrive to arrest him. In one account, he hangs himself following the betrayal. In Acts, he buys a field with the silver he had received and dies when he falls into it and his bowels burst open.

There are two theories about the motive for Judas' betrayal. The first suggests that he was driven by greed, the second that he had become disillusioned with Jesus' pacifism, preferring a more militant response to Roman oppression. If this were true, then Judas might have joined Jesus' movement in the hope that he would inspire a popular rebellion, in which case Judas himself might have felt betrayed by Jesus' gospel of love.

29: THE CRY ON THE CROSS

Crucifixion was among the cruelest forms of execution practiced in the ancient world. It had long been used by the Assyrians and Persians when the Romans adopted it as a punishment for slaves and rebels. Roman citizens could only be crucified if they had committed treason. The fact that crucifixion was used to punish Jesus suggests that his claim to be the Jewish messiah was interpreted by the authorities as an act of rebellion against Rome. In any event, Jesus was sentenced and executed by Romans and not by Jews, as many Christians have supposed. The ruling council at Jerusalem may have had its own reasons for wanting Jesus dead, but they would have been forbidden from taking matters into their own hands. Rome executed prisoners for its own purposes, and in accordance with its own laws.

According to the gospels, the crucifixion of Jesus occurs as follows. The night before his execution, he is betrayed by Judas Iscariot in the Garden of Gethsemane, after which he is made to answer for himself before both Jewish and Roman authorities. He is flogged and mocked by being forced to wear a purple robe and a crown of thorns, both symbolic of kingship. He is then made to carry his own cross to Golgotha, "the place of the skull," so named because it was an execution ground. There he is nailed to a cross and placed between two thieves who have likewise been sentenced to die.

From the cross Jesus tells the disciple John to care for Mary, his mother. He also begs forgiveness for his enemies, praying, "Father, forgive them, for they know not what they do." One of the thieves mocks him, asking why, if he is truly the Christ, he cannot save himself and them. But the other thief rebukes him, concluding, "For we receive the due reward of our deeds: but this man hath done nothing amiss." He then asks to be remembered by Jesus when he comes into his Father's kingdom. Jesus replies, "Today shalt thou be with me in paradise."

Jesus' cry "My God, my God, why hast thou forsaken me?" occurs at the very end, after which he dies. Mark offers no explanation for why Jesus should have felt abandoned by God at the very end. However, Psalm 22 suggests a possible answer.

That Psalm begins, "My God, my God, why hast thou forsaken me? why art thou so far from helping me, and from the words of my roaring?" What follows is a classical lament in which the speaker praises God for answering the prayers of Israel in the past but bemoans his current condition. "But I am a worm, and no man," he declares, "a reproach of men, and despised of the people." He is laughed at to the point of scorn by those who ask him why the God who finds him so delightful does not intervene to save him. A visceral sense of the speaker's suffering is described when he tells us that his heart is like melted wax within him, his strength has dried up like a potsherd, and his tongue has stuck to the roof of his mouth. He is in such painful physical agony that he can count each of his bones. "They pierced my hands and my feet," he says finally, and adds that lots have been cast for who shall take possession of his clothes.

It is possible to find in Psalm 22 not only a description of what it must have felt like to be crucified, but also a number of specific parallels to the circumstances of Jesus' crucifixion, for the first thief mocks him in like manner, and the Roman soldiers cast lots for his clothes. However, this is not where Psalm 22 ends.

In the second half of the psalm, the speaker makes an impassioned plea for deliverance that contains many images of renewal and regeneration. In spite of his suffering, the speaker tells of the ongoing "seed of Jacob" and predicts that people throughout the world will recognize the glory of God and seek it: "All the ends of the world shall remember and turn unto the Lord: and all the kindreds of the nations shall worship before thee."

In all, Psalm 22 suggests a journey through emptiness and despair that nevertheless ends with a mood of rebirth or resurrection, because that inner desolation is discovered to be part of a timeless journey in which humanity and all its ideas about God are always dying and being reborn.

30: THE GATELESS GATE

The book of Revelation, sometimes also called the Apocalypse of St. John the Divine, begins when Christ sends an angel to John (not the apostle but a later figure) on the island of Patmos and commands him to warn the church of trials to come. John travels to heaven in a vision and sees God sitting on a throne. God holds a scroll with seven seals, which can be opened only by the Lamb (symbolic of Jesus). The Lamb opens the seals one after another, and with each seal a great judgment is released upon the world.

In subsequent chapters, there ensues a battle of cosmic proportions in which the Lamb and 144,000 of his followers fight the seven-headed beast who is Satan's representative on earth. Satan himself is overcome in the end and there follows a thousand-year period of peace, at the end of which a new heaven and earth are born and the Divine City, the "New Jerusalem," descends from the heavens.

In the end, John awakes from his vision, and the book of Revelation comes to a close with Jesus telling readers that he will come quickly to initiate the events that have been described therein.

APPENDIX B

Forming a Weekly Study Group

How to Believe in God (Whether You Believe in Religion or Not) was inspired by a weekly study group that began meeting in January 2000. Apart from the two rules and the brief outline of our spiritual process mentioned in Chapter 7, "Jacob and the Angel," little instruction is required to form such a group. For those wanting to hold meetings of their own, however, it may be helpful to observe the following format:

- Arrange the chairs in a circle so that each person's face is visible to every other person.
- Begin with a period of silence, preferably in dim light, during which members are free to pray or meditate as they like.
- At the beginning of each discussion, read the passage you selected the week before. In Woodstock, we usually read a single chapter from the Bible at the beginning of each meeting,

dividing the number of verses in the chapter by the number of participants that night so that each person gets to read a few verses out loud.

- Allow members to speak when, and if, they desire, imposing no fixed structure on the manner or order of speaking.
- At the end of each meeting, agree on the passage for discussion the following week. You may discover that it is simpler to read an entire book from the Bible together, chapter by chapter, than to have to select a new passage every week, but there should be no rules governing the selection process, except that a majority of members must agree on the passage selected.
- Finally, remember that the spiritual intimacy fostered week after week by such a group—both with God and with one another—is what leads to spiritual transformation. Any words or actions that increase that intimacy are, as a rule, good for the group and for the individual.

For those wishing to find out more about *How to Believe in God* and the group that inspired it, please visit our Web site at www.Buddhist BibleStudy.com.

ABOUT THE AUTHOR

CLARK STRAND is a Buddhist teacher and the director of the Koans of the Bible Study Group, an ecumenical, interreligious spiritual community. A former Zen Buddhist monk, he is a contributing editor of *Tricycle: The Buddhist Review* and has written a variety of books and aritcles on spiritual practice. He lives in the Catskill Mountains with his wife and children.